PROFIT FROM THE PROFIT

PROFIT FROM THE PROFIT

THE PAST, PRESENT & FUTURE OF DIVIDEND GROWTH INVESTING

DAVID L. BAHNSEN

Post Hill
PRESS

A POST HILL PRESS BOOK
ISBN: 979-8-89565-230-5
ISBN (eBook): 979-8-89565-231-2

Profit from the Profit:
The Past, Present & Future of Dividend Growth Investing

Cover design by Mina Widmer

Post Hill Press
New York • Nashville
posthillpress.com

Published in the United States of America
1 2 3 4 5 6 7 8 9 10

This book is dedicated to Tom Bonds, my friend and brother for life. (Proverbs 18:24)

If the greatest yield one gets from friendship is shared experiences—both trials and triumphs—then I have received more dividends from my friendship with Tom than I will ever get from my portfolio.

I have profited greatly from the model Tom has set in terms of love for his family, personal discipline, and the resilience life calls for at times.

More than anything else, though, Tom's care for me when I needed it most has been a dividend with an incalculable ROI. And I am never, ever selling that stock.

TABLE OF CONTENTS

FOREWORD
by John Mauldin

WE HAVE ALL HAD THE experience of reading a book that has a profound impact on us. Something in it either changes our understanding of the world around us or reveals things to us that we simply had not understood before. Sometimes, it even changes the way we conduct our lives and our businesses.

David L. Bahnsen's *The Case for Dividend Growth: Investing in a Post-Crisis World* changed the basic investment philosophy that I had, generally successfully, held for thirty years. I will admit that the 1970s, the crash of 1987, the ups and downs of the 1990s, and the crash of the early 2000s, followed by the Great Recession, made me very comfortable with my choice of using a diversified portfolio of alternative investments. Not every choice was a winner every year, but the result was a reasonable return with far less volatility than the stock market.

I was, and still am, concerned about the potential for a serious generational crisis later this decade—one that could have a profound impact on all markets. This concern became more personal after the events of 2020 and my realization that my portfolio was far too complex for my younger wife, or even a trustee, to handle if something were to happen to me. While alternative investments have a place, they have to be monitored continually, and that is no easy task.

I have had the luxury of being David's friend for fifteen years. We met on the set of CNBC's *Fast Money* in 2011, and I was impressed with him. After the show, I introduced myself and casually said, "I recognize the name Bahnsen. I published a book by a theologian named Greg Bahnsen." David replied that Greg was his father. We began corresponding regularly and meeting for what became frequent dinners with a few friends. (I think he was just happy to find somebody in finance who knew what presuppositionalism is.)

While I bought *The Case for Dividend Growth* when it came out in 2019, I began to read it later in 2020. It forced me to rethink my views on how to get through a coming crisis with my portfolio intact and, more importantly, how to ensure that my wife, Shane, would be taken care of. The worst thing I could do would be to pass on a complex portfolio with no one to monitor it and maintain it wisely.

This realization triggered some deep conversations with David. First, he made me realize that while there may indeed be an impending crisis, we don't know what shape it will take. Further, he encouraged my optimistic belief that "this too shall pass." To paraphrase Warren Buffett, don't bet against America.

Then, I watched as David's dividend portfolio went down in certain market downturns, but less than the overall market with quicker recovery—just as similar dividend growth portfolios had in every other crisis for the past hundred years. And those dividends just kept compounding.

Those familiar with my writing know that I am not a fan of static portfolios or index funds. When analyzing how

David and his investment team manage their dividend growth portfolio, I realize that it is anything but fixed. They constantly reevaluate each stock in what is typically a thirty-five-stock portfolio, harvesting profits when a stock has exceeded its ability to deliver a meaningful dividend and removing a company when it appears that its dividend is in jeopardy. It is a thoughtful, disciplined approach to portfolio management.

While I don't want to dampen the thunder you will encounter while reading this book, I have become convinced that a dividend growth portfolio should be the core of my long-term investment strategy. Not an addition, but the core.

The companies that make up David's dividend growth portfolio will still be around in 2035 and beyond. Even though these are primarily US companies, many of them make more than half their profits internationally, making this a globally diversified portfolio.

And as David sometimes cheekily reminds me, a crisis is far from guaranteed. What if we, as a country, deal with our debt issues and resolve our current political contretemps? Luckily, a dividend growth portfolio will fare well, crisis or no. It exemplifies the modern iteration of Graham and Dodd value investing.

While this book updates the data to this year, it is more than just a recap of statistics—it is deeply philosophical with much to meditate on. For those interested in the science of investment, reading this book will be a journey of intellectual joy.

While the data reinforces the primacy of dividend growth investing, David also brilliantly introduces us to an understanding not only of how we invest, but also the reasons *why* we invest and the rationale behind portfolio construction. This book serves as the *sine qua non* on dividend growth investing and why it should be in your portfolio repertoire, but it will give you a profound sense of enlightenment on the very nature of investing as well.

And since David is too humble, let me supply his brief biography. His father was one of the most philosophically rigorous minds I have ever met. The apple did not fall far from the tree. Unfortunately, Greg passed away while David was a very young adult, and because theologians don't typically build college trust funds, David had to go to work early. He found his passion in managing money and investments and now runs an investment advisory company that will soon see its assets grow past $10 billion. The company currently has twelve offices and around a hundred employees. And while dividend growth portfolios are at the company's core, it also allocates a significant amount to alternative investments, real estate, and boring bonds.

While I have some small knowledge of alternative investments, David and his team are some of the best I have ever worked with. They are not just an investment management firm; they build customized portfolios for each client, perform tailored financial planning, full tax strategy and preparation, and run family offices. They are a true wealth management firm. David has that unique entrepreneurial ability to attract, keep, and motivate a team of professionals that meets his personal, ethical, and moral standards.

I highly recommend you subscribe to his daily newsletter, *Dividend Café*, especially the Friday commentary. Plus, you should tune in to his weekly podcast for *National Review*, "Capital Record." He is regularly listed as one of America's top wealth managers by *Barron's*, *Forbes*, and more, and appears on financial TV multiple times per week. He is one of the most disciplined individuals I've ever met, both intellectually and in his daily personal life.

On a personal note, I couldn't wish for a greater friend. While my plan is to live a great deal longer, I take comfort in the fact that The Bahnsen Group will make sure that Shane will always be in good hands.

Your sleeping better at night analyst,

John Mauldin

INTRODUCTION

"The very attention we place on rising dividends puts us squarely in the position of 'owners' of a company... [not] a gift of the market or luck... but it is the logical and inevitable result of investing in a company that is actually doing well enough, in the real world, to both pay dividends and to increase them on a regular basis."

—Lowell Miller

I DO NOT RECALL IF I thought *The Case for Dividend Growth* would be my final published word on the topic of dividend growth investing. When I wrote it in 2018 and published it in 2019, I believed that history would continue as it always had for investors, spurring events that cause both positive and negative reactions in capital assets. The book covered a fair amount of history, and I am sure I was not so arrogant as to think it would foresee all future events. In light of this, it seems appropriate to update and refine its message to reflect newer circumstances and developments, roughly eight years later.

That said, that book addressed timeless principles that are always applicable to the practice of investing. If I stand by the principle-based arguments of that book, why bring a new dividend growth book to market? Sure, the period of time since the publication of *The Case for Dividend Growth* saw the COVID-19 moment, the transition from the FAANG era[1] to the Magnificent Seven era,[2] and ample geopolitical tumult, but when I wrote *The Case for Dividend Growth*, I never intended to rewrite it for every news cycle or market era. A major argument for dividend growth investing is that it "works" through ever-changing news events, market leadership, and investment rotations. Its particular benefits may vary from one season to the next, but the efficacy of dividend growth investing is, by definition, not undermined by the way the wind blows. Why, then, write a new book eight years later? Is my prior book obsolete? Have new criticisms surfaced that warrant response? Has my position changed? Am I desperate for something to do with my ample free time?

The answers to the last few questions are all "no," with a more emphatic version of "no" to that last one. The philosophy explicated in *The Case for Dividend Growth* has not

1 FAANG was a popular acronym after 2013 for a group of new technology companies that would come to represent the decade's most significant market movers and cultural icons: Facebook, Amazon, Apple, Netflix, and Google. The term was popularized by Jim Cramer on CNBC.

2 The term Magnificent Seven (Mag 7 for short) was the brainchild of Michael Hartnett, chief investment strategist at Bank of America. New phraseology was needed to replace FAANG with the ascendance in the early 2020s of Nvidia, Tesla, and Microsoft. Those three names were merged with FAANG constituents Apple, Alphabet, Meta, and Amazon. The lesser market capitalization and much smaller profit generation of Netflix left it out.

changed, and I believe the book has stood up quite well in its fundamental arguments. As far as my professional and personal convictions about dividend growth investing go, I am content with my 2019 book standing on its claims and arguments in perpetuity.

Profit from the Profit is not meant to replace *The Case for Dividend Growth* or to alter any of its arguments. It is, instead, intended to expand on those arguments, update data where appropriate, engage with arguments that were not discussed in the prior book, and generally improve and refine the case for dividend growth investing. Some arguments will prove redundant simply because many factors and arguments are the same in 2026 as they were in 2019. Some new subjects are covered in this book, either because they are newer formulations in my own mind, or because I feel more equipped to bring them to public light than I did during the past decade. My intellectual journey as a professional investor did not end in 2019 and my own beliefs on this subject contain even deeper convictions now than they did then. It is my earnest hope that this work will capture all that was important about *The Case for Dividend Growth* while adding new truths, revelations, and formulations that make *Profit from the Profit* an even more, well, profitable read.

Dividend growth investing was and is now countercultural, in contrast to the allure of "trading" one's way to wealth (preferably, quickly). While the end of a given market cycle can generally only be called with the gift of hindsight, the belief that very popular (and successful) companies can see their price compound indefinitely at rates far higher than the market remains deeply ingrained in the minds of many investors. And outside of the appeal of trading, or "hot dot" stocks, there is certainly the time-tested belief that one can merely "ignore it all" with a passive index approach—and ride out the up and down volatility of the market. Interfering through active dividend growth management is contrary to the passive approach that has worked for many investors. Many investors get impatient: avoiding hot dot momentum plays is anathema to those who believe that a dividend lags behind the quickness with which the stock market "normally" generates staggering returns. I am well aware of why these investors reject dividend growth investing. In this book, I intend to address their concerns. But I have no delusions that dividend growth investing will become "trendy." This philosophy of investing requires too much discipline and is far too connected to the core of human nature to ever become popular with the masses. I consider this, counterintuitively, one of its most compelling features. Any system that requires the approval of the crowd to work is vulnerable, and dividend growth investing is, and always has been, completely disinterested in its own popularity.

I began *The Case for Dividend Growth* with the argument that first brought me to dividend growth investing: that all investing is, fundamentally, about cash flow. Someone parts with money and wants to get it back with a return—period. That "getting it back" may be all at once or over a long period of time. It may be for one's own use or for the use of a charity or spouse or grandchildren, but it is, ultimately, for the investor. One parts with money so that one eventually gets it back.

The argument that, "No, I can let it compound forever. I don't need the money back. I don't need income—I just want growth," doesn't contradict what I have said. That "growth" only becomes useful when it is monetized for a use. Many investors may not need the fruit from the tree they've planted, but the tree is there for cash flow—whether it be a realized gain in the future, a lump sum purchase, a steady withdrawal of value, a stream of income, or some combination of the above. There are two major variables here: the timeline of when money is wanted or needed, and the manner in which it is needed. The timeline for a return of cash may be short (such as when buying a house) or it may be long (such as when leaving money to the grandchildren's inheritance). The manner of return may be a lump sum (say, buying a boat) or it may be periodic (think retirement income). And yes, some expenses may span both categories (such as the medium-term goal of college education paid out in four years). But the x-axis is a timeline for investors, and the y-axis is a manner of return of cash.

This made me realize that a significant amount of contemporary investment debate is misguided. Confusion between "growth" and "income" was creating false binaries that led people to make significant mistakes. A stock that has gone up for a long time might be a great thing for an investor with a certain timeline and risk appetite and no particular current cash flow need, but there are still some "mechanics" at play—the short- versus long-term and lump sum versus periodic dynamic of eventual monetization. Perhaps "unrealized gains" were a better way to achieve future monetization needs (whether they emerged as a lump sum or periodically), but the existence of an "unrealized gain" did not represent a new investment objective. Investing boils down to a timeline and a manner of cash return. Once the conversation is framed accurately (with enough nuance around timeline and mechanism), I have never heard of any investment objective that could not be reduced to some form of cash return.

Of course, timeline and cash mechanics are not the only things that matter to an investor. Risk matters. Volatility matters. (Note: these two are not the same thing.) Tax efficiency matters. Liquidity matters. All these factors and more play into what makes for an optimal portfolio for a given investor. One of the reasons my firm customizes portfolio allocations to each individual client is that we have not found that people exist as members of just three different "buckets." There is enough variance in comfort levels, timelines, objectives, and other factors that reducing one's portfolio to bucket A, bucket B, or bucket C seems, well, lazy—and also a poor service to clients.

At issue in this book is not if asset allocation is necessary for each investor. It is, of course. Dividend growth equities constitute the portion of one's portfolio that pursues a return well above the rate of inflation, that is intended to compound capital for accumulators (those with a longer-term horizon), and that sustains a growing withdrawal rate for those who are periodic withdrawers of capital (whether immediately or down the line). I am convinced that dividend growth investing creates a better result for accumulators and withdrawers of capital than any other risk strategy available to the masses I have studied.

The accusation should be, at this point, that I am, quite literally, "talking my book." At press time, my company manages in excess of $9 billion, more than half of which is invested in dividend growth equities. We actively manage a fund that trades on the New York Stock Exchange and mirrors our dividend growth strategy.[3] My personal US stock port-

3 See The Bahnsen Group, "TBG DIV Focus," www.tbgdividendgrowth.com, for more information and disclosures on ticker TBG.

folio entirely reflects our dividend growth strategy, and all of the partners and advisors at The Bahnsen Group can say the same. We eat what we cook. That said, it is important to get the sequence right when we refer to me "talking my book." I did not create a dividend growth portfolio and then decide I needed convictions to justify that approach. I had convictions backing up the approach, *and so then created* the dividend growth portfolio. Yes, what I espouse in this book (and my prior one) matches what we do with client money (and my own), but that is because we believe in it. I didn't write this book to match what I do when managing money. The way I manage money reflects what I believe (which is captured in this book).

I intend to reiterate the argument that dividend growth creates a reinvestment compounding machine that is mathematically miraculous, underrated, and potent. I will contrast this accumulation strategy with other popular approaches, both to compare their records and to evaluate their respective risks. I will examine the allure of certain investing trends over the past few decades and evaluate why the hype has not matched the results. And I will restate the argument that only dividend growth turns the hardest part of public equity investing (drawdowns and inevitable volatility) into an automatic moneymaking feature, not a bug.

The question of withdrawal strategy has become one of primary importance for an increasing number of investors. Too many retirees have no defined withdrawal strategy at all, which means they *do* have a withdrawal strategy: "I'll take it when I need it and hope it all works out." The lesson I learned from the 2000–2002 bear market and the 2000–2009 decade remains real, repeatable, and existential: how an investment performs over time is irrelevant if there is not enough of that investment left for that compounding to matter. Dividend growth investing remains an impenetrable way to protect the sustainability of a withdrawal stream in the inevitable reality of bad markets. Prolonged bull markets do not change this fact or this math—they just dull people to how pivotally important this message is.

I remain committed to the belief that dividend growth is a superior strategy for identifying superior companies. I have never believed in dividend growth merely because I want the dividend; rather, I receive the dividend because I want the company to be able to pay it, protect it, and grow it. The dividend becomes a benefit (the received cash) and something signifying a benefit (the quality of enterprise) all at once. As I said in the title of Chapter Three of my prior book making this case, we don't buy the stock to get the dividend—we buy the dividend to get the stock!

And I believe, with strong empirical evidence, that this approach is available without having to sacrifice long-term returns. The case that "dividend growth is more inherently defensive and is probably better for retirees, but I want me some aggressive growth!" falters under scrutiny. Not only have dividend growth equities created better results over long-term horizons than popular alternatives, but they have done so with far less volatility, drawdown, and testing of emotional endurance.

I continue to believe that dividends represent the form of capital return to shareholders that most respects and rewards the shareholder, and will devote new resources and attention to that argument. If this book can provide any improved clarity over the last, I pray it will be on this point. All we are ever debating with this point is *what companies ought to do with profits.* One can argue for the merit of companies that don't have profits or for the merit of guessing which companies don't have profits today but will have profits tomorrow. Regardless of the way one chooses to invest, they still, eventually, have to answer this question: "How should a company reward its shareholders?" Profits are a given for successful companies (eventually), and the case I make in this book is that dividend growth investing allows risk-takers who only own a minority interest in the business to optimally *profit from those profits.*

The issue of tax efficiency was addressed in my prior book, but here I will offer a more extensive argument about the dividend growth tax reality: it is a benefit to the underlying investor. Refuting the tax argument against dividend growth will be easier than many believe, as you will soon see.

One thing this book will do that was not discussed at all in *The Case for Dividend Growth* is look at the "macro" fears driving many doomsdayers. This attitude does not offer a critique of dividend growth, per se, but rather any form of risk-taking. I intend to give a sober, judicious, historical, and charitable assessment of why that concern is wrong, and how it is best mitigated in the portfolio construction process.

I will spend more time in this book than in the past one "putting this into practice," analyzing how dividend growth fits into a complete asset allocation, why we do not write covered calls against dividend-growing companies we want to own, and how the fundamental, bottom-up process of assessing dividend growth sustainability must always be a "both/and" of qualitative and quantitative components. We are not trying to create "do-it-yourself" dividend growth investors, but we do want to give a look under the hood at the decisions we have made in managing money this way, what went into those decisions, lessons we have learned, and how to mitigate the inevitability of fallibility.

And for those who make it to the appendix at the end of this book, I want to do something I wish I had done in the first book: *offer a theological case for dividend growth investing.* I have never been afraid of wearing my identity on my sleeve, and I am a worldview-conscious man of faith who believes in transcendent principles as part of my Christian convictions, which I think are intimately connected to this subject. I am not arguing that dividend growth investing is "spiritual" and other forms of investing are somehow "unspiritual." Rather, for those interested, I merely want to show how "yield" and the "growth of yield" fits into the Christian worldview. Even if the subject or faith commitments are of no interest to you, I believe you'll find the appendix treatment valuable.

Yes, a lot has happened since *The Case for Dividend Growth* was published in 2019. What was true then—and remains true today—is that there is an investment strategy available to the masses that taps into profits, aligns the managers of businesses with investors in those businesses, and secures the financial objectives of those who pursue this successfully in a multitude of outcomes and cash flow mechanics. That investment strategy really does come down to positioning oneself to profit from the profit.

CHAPTER ONE

AN INVESTMENT PHILOSOPHY

"Modern formulations are necessary even in defense of very ancient truths. Not because of any alleged anachronisms in the old ideas… but because the idiom of life is always changing, and we need to say things in such a way as to get inside the vibrations of modern life."

—Bill Buckley

"The single greatest edge is a patient and informed mind."

—Howard Marks

I HAVE NEVER BEEN IN denial about the fact that many of my own investment biases and practices formed when I began professionally managing money. My experience as a stock market investor in the second half of the 1990s taught me some painful lessons, and beginning a career in professional money management right in the aftermath of the tech boom implosion created experiences and insights I have not forgotten. This is a good thing.

I am sure there are many gold bugs still around whose first experience with investment pain and macro challenges was the 1970s. Bond investors who began their careers with spiking interest rates carry a permanent (and entirely rational) fear of higher yields. Japanese investors from the 1980s don't need any lectures about a "long-term approach"—any risk assets they bought in the 1980s were deflated away over the "long term" of thirty (plus) years. Those who bought index funds in 2009 have a pretty reasonable basis for feeling good about the risk-adjusted results that "buy and hold" passivity has generated. Big-cap tech investors in that same period have been raised on "what goes up always goes higher, and barely ever goes lower." Our first experiences influence our investment precepts forever. It is human nature.

But this is very different than having an investment *philosophy*. I would imagine that most people's investment *strategies* have been formed either by the negative experience of something going very wrong, or the positive experience of something going very right. Strategy is far too often based on experience rather than something more intellectually defensible.

My first decade managing money saw big cap growth get hammered, dividend growth do quite well, passive index investing break even (bookended by two nasty bear markets), and interest rates plunged toward zero even as the largest population base in history headed to retirement. Is it possible that I based the investment strategy of dividend growth on the experiences of my early career? There is no point in denying that these experiences were formative and foundational, but I can say that dividend growth is, for me, a by-product of an investment philosophy. The commitments and beliefs that make up that philosophy were certainly inspired, in part, by the experiences of my early career, but I have made it my life's work to transcend my own experience in formulating strategy, and root our commitment to and execution of dividend growth investment in a more holistic philosophy.

Many investors are committed to a strategy that would have destroyed their financial goals in the first decade of my career. This intransigence is self-defeating. This is not the same as admitting to PTSD about a difficult market period, which can be hard—but crucial—to overcome. It is an admission that they have adopted an investment strategy that has worked in one investment period, but would not have worked in another. I do not mean here merely that it "has been up" but at another point "would have been down"—that is true of all investment strategies. I mean, "the investment strategy would have failed in reaching its goals." I find this outcome unacceptable. The lessons I learned in watching dot-com blow up, or seeing it take sixteen years for the Nasdaq to recover, or observing the damage of excessive margin debt in purchasing the underlying securities that collateralize the debt, were not just that "things can go bad." The far more consequential and personal lesson was that the "retiree cannot support his withdrawal rate anymore," or that the "accumulator has to adjust quality of life expectations in the future." This happened to millions of people, and it happened for reasons that go far beyond a deficient strategy.

I am guilty of being permanently influenced by the lessons I learned early in my career, but I believe that those lessons did not result in mere timidity or hesitation. They allowed me, and in some ways forced me, to more comprehensively evaluate *why* I believe what I believe.

GOING DEEPER

In the summer of 2025, I was interviewed by economist John Mauldin, a dear friend (and the author of this book's foreword). In the course of that interview, John and I delved into the genesis of my commitment to dividend growth investing.[1] John had an insider's understanding of what I would say because he is one of the few people involved in my investment world who knew my late father, Dr. Greg L. Bahnsen. My answer to John (which I subsequently turned into a commentary for his *Thoughts from the Frontline* newsletter) connected two worlds for me: a framework of understanding with which I was raised and an application regarding investment strategy.

John and I first met on set at CNBC more than fifteen years ago. John had been involved in the publication of some of my father's scholarly materials back in the 1980s. As Greg and David Bahnsen share a distinctive last name (according to ChatGPT, one of every 2,603,625 people has it—so 3,000 of 8 billion people), it was not hard for John to guess that we might be related. Though John and I immediately developed a friendship of our own, his familiarity with my dad and my upbringing spurred his question. Why one believes in a certain investment philosophy can be an innocuous inquiry, but I think that John knew it would prove to be loaded.

I have to bring up my father to explain why I think investing requires a distinct philosophy. Greg Bahnsen was a

1 The Bahnsen Group, *Why I Entrust My Money with The Bahnsen Group*, Vimeo, https://vimeo.com/1111361999.

Christian intellectual whose doctoral work at the University of Southern California focused on epistemology—the study of the nature and limits of human knowledge. He had an uncanny ability to ask what was real (metaphysics), how we know things (epistemology), and how we should then live (ethics), *in all domains of human experience.* He took philosophy very seriously, questioning how we know what we know, and what we ought to do about it.

So, what does this have to do with investment portfolios? How does the curiosity that has driven philosophers for millennia influence asset allocation? Is there a benefit to constructing a philosophical framework for one's portfolio management decisions? An even better question may be: Is there *really* anyone who manages money without *some* investment philosophy? Does a lack of awareness of one's governing framework mean one lacks one? Just as my late father taught me that all people have a worldview they use to critically assess the world and interpret human experience, all investors have some philosophical framework, some network of beliefs that dictates the decisions they make in allocating capital.

The question is not whether there is a philosophy at play; rather, the question is how thoughtful, coherent, and defensible that philosophy may be. Of course, a cogent investment philosophy does not relieve us of the burden of diligent execution and wise decision-making. But diligent execution and wise decision-making are futile if not rooted in a coherent investment philosophy. In addition to coherence, conviction can only come from self-awareness and critical scrutiny, which ought to be table stakes for serious asset allocators.

Bottom line: *If someone invests capital without knowing what he believes, he is unlikely to be good at investing capital.*

He may very well enjoy seasons of strong returns, but sustaining results that support one's long-term financial objectives is far less likely if decision-making is disconnected from a cogent foundation.

In asset management, an investor can often benefit from circumstances outside of his or her control (good luck is as real as bad luck). That said, positive results are far more sustainable when tethered to a solid philosophy, leaving investors much more likely to preserve their sanity.

Having a discernible investment philosophy when one invests money is a necessary—but not sufficient—condition for sustainable success. Not all investment philosophies are created equal. Many people believe that the key to investing capital is to follow trends, chase momentum, and use their own instincts to determine what markets will do next. It is, I believe, a flawed philosophy, but it *is* a philosophy. Presumably, those who believe and practice such convictions have a reason for hewing to them. I have had many conversations with adherents of such a belief system where their own convictions and biases were defended and presented well (albeit unpersuasively).

PHILOSOPHY VERSUS STRATEGY

First, an important distinction is in order. An investment *strategy* and an investment *philosophy* are not the same thing. A strategy is a *plan* that includes factors for decision-making. Strategy ought to be tethered to a philosophy, but they are not the same. The philosophy behind a strategy seeks to answer *why* a strategy will work as intended. Philosophy reflects the presuppositions and conceptual beliefs that someone brings to the decision-making process; strategy reflects how one responds to those beliefs.

"Buy and hold" is an investment strategy. The philosophy behind it is easily elucidated:

- A collection of companies will experience earnings growth over time because of how markets work. Earnings growth and previous market experience are highly likely to repeat themselves.
- The goal for investors is compounding, which is threatened by selection risk. Attempting to assess winners and losers in the market is difficult.
- Timing risk is an even more potent threat as it interrupts compounding and asks humans to make predictions that are very difficult to get right.
- The future is likely to look like the past and markets are reasonably efficient.
- The collective of diversified market activity is sufficient for investor returns. The individual realities of particular underlying companies do not drive results as much as what a collective market does.

This mindset takes these philosophical commitments, most of which are fair enough, and builds a strategy of passive index investing where the mantra is "buy and hold."

Momentum investing is not an exception to the assertion that all strategies are connected to some philosophy. That said, I am not convinced many people have thought through the presuppositions behind momentum investing. I find the conviction that "what goes up will continue to go up" spurious, but many believe in a strategy of momentum the same way they believe in the laws of gravity (sometimes even outright connecting the two).

My intent is not to critique competing philosophies of investment (though I will do so somewhat). Much like the critical analysis we do for many serious topics, a prudent investment manager must examine the philosophy that underlies varying investment strategies, and determine his or her own investment philosophy. This is the way a sturdy, lasting building is constructed: on a foundation that has been challenged, analyzed, and found formidable.

THE DEFAULT APPROACH OF OUR DAY

When I entered the investment business as the son of a philosopher, I was flummoxed by the lack of a foundation in so much of what passed as investment strategy. Some of the greatest minds on Wall Street (dealmakers in private equity or M&A investment bankers) are intellectually complacent about why a market functions the way it does. I am sure there are surgeons out there who are incredibly good at performing a certain operation without really understanding why the operation functions the way it does (but truth be told, I wouldn't want that person operating on me). When it comes to decisions about allocating your own capital, let alone the capital of others (as professional asset allocators do), such intellectual complacency persistently leads to a destructive outcome: abandoning strategy because it lacks foundation. But why would someone abandon his investment strategy just because he couldn't philosophically defend it? Because all strategies vacillate in performance, and without a foundation, one is liable to act emotionally and reactively. This is the *de facto* investment philosophy of most people: invest in whatever just finished working.

That may not seem like a very coherent philosophy—because it isn't. But it is what undergirds most of the investing public's strategy.

A PHILOSOPHY OF ECONOMICS

My investment philosophy has, at its core, the belief in human action as the driver of wealth creation. This belief stems from a theological normative for me: that humans were made in the image of God, and, consequently, are co-creators with Him. Out of this doctrine of creation, I find an anthropology that explains markets and offers a view of the human person that is coherent, explanatory, and aspirational. If mankind was "created to create" and imbued with rationality, creativity, and responsibility, markets exist without imposition. Indeed, there is a long tradition in classical economics of viewing the human person as the proactive agent in economic activity.

I believe humans act out of their own God-given instincts, reason, and rational faculties (and yes, as image-bearers of God), and markets emerge from these traits. Humans have their own subjective preferences, goals, and abilities, but they act as social animals, cooperating with others to survive and thrive. Every advancement in standards of living, investable development, and bit of material progress has come about as a by-product of human action. This invites discussions of the role that human action plays in driving the policy ramifications of economic behavior (it serves as the framework for the Austrian school, for example, which prioritized human agency over central planning). It also has investment implications for sources of "risk premia" (excess return beyond a safe and universal liquid asset).

Seeing the innovation, creativity, and productivity of the human person as the bedrock of economic calculation centers my investment philosophy on bottom-up activity that creates value. I do not see wealth as created by chance, nor do I see gaming arbitrage opportunities in perpetuity as feasible. I see human beings producing goods and services as the sole source of wealth creation since the beginning of time. This causes me to seek investment *strategies* that follow from an investment *philosophy* recognizing human action as the foundation of economics.

A PHILOSOPHY OF PORTFOLIO CONSTRUCTION

Nothing I have said so far is systematic, let alone comprehensive. It is the beginning of what one may consider "investment philosophy fodder." The systematic presentation of that philosophy is the subject of this book.

Let me begin the presentation of my philosophy by laying out a handful of tenets that serve as the bedrock of my philosophy and underlie the arguments of the pages to come. These basic precepts have led me to the strategy of dividend growth and are founded on these beliefs:

- Human action drives economic activity.
- Wealth creation is not speculative; it comes from the organic activity of profit-seeking enterprises that learn from failure, take risks, and create goods and services that meet the needs of humanity.

- Macroeconomic conditions impact the conditions of entrepreneurial endeavors but do not supersede them.
- The human tendency to follow the crowd leads to overcrowding that intensifies risk in some investment spheres and underinvestment that magnifies opportunity in others. These risks and opportunities do not always manifest on our preferred timelines.
- Past mathematical relationships between different asset classes won't necessarily continue because human activity is dynamic. Therefore, the mathematical relationships between asset classes are dynamic. In other words, expectations that "gold and silver are supposed to trade in XYZ ratio to one another" are hogwash.
- An investment that has no internal rate of return is called a "speculative investment." An internal rate of return is the yield that comes either from the price of time, like interest, or the creation of value, like profits.
- Human beings are innovative and capable but can also be self-interested and corrupt. The idea is to find systems where there is optimal alignment between business managers and business owners.

From private equity to venture capital to small-cap investing to emerging markets equity, and yes, to our bread-and-butter belief in public equity dividend growth, we at The Bahnsen Group have a strong bias toward the bottom-up activity of business innovation, action, and calculation. The source of risk premium is the profit-making activity of human beings. We are not looking at relative value arbitrage of one traditional relationship to another. Those econometric and quantitative strategies may work (temporarily) for some, but we can't be motivated by anything as much as we are by business enterprise—the production of goods and services that profitably meet the needs of humanity. Many different strategies exist within that basic premise, but it is our North Star. It has also become rather controversial.

I have habitually avoided significant investment pain, not because I always picked the best strategies but because I was raised to evaluate investment advice with a critical eye. My internal critiques have, time and time again, caused me to be skeptical of things that did, in fact, warrant skepticism (shiny objects, momentum fads, unsustainable pipe dreams, endeavors devoid of human ingenuity and freedom, and on and on).

It has created a burden for me and my team to rigorously and vigorously question, challenge, and defend our own presuppositions and beliefs about investing. I do not suggest that every investor needs to geek out on philosophy before placing a trade. But I will lay out a series of questions worthy of being asked by anyone who holds or manages an investment portfolio:

- Why do you own what you own?
- Why do you believe what you own makes up a cohesive investment strategy?
- What do you know of human experience and knowledge that validates this strategy?
- What do you know of human experience and knowledge that might contradict it?

These four questions are not comprehensive, but they're a great starting point.

Questions about reality, human experience, nature, and truth have existed for thousands of years. Some have provided better frameworks for cogent understanding than others. (This was the inheritance my father left me). But sincere intellectual curiosity is a precondition for almost all consequential knowledge, and a key driver of investment success.

A PHILOSOPHY OF BEHAVIOR

I understand that people are not reading this investment book to hear my expressions of appreciation for my own dad, Greg Bahnsen. That said, the universal truths I learned from him became the foundation of my investment philosophy.

Greg Bahnsen's doctoral dissertation was on self-deception, with an epistemological and apologetical focus. He believed that human beings can know truths but suppress them under certain conditions, which leads to decisions and behaviors that go against God's design for our lives. We do not believe "P" and "not P" at the same time—we simply suppress one belief when desirable or necessary. His focus here was apologetical—he did not want to argue people into a belief if their challenge was less intellectual and more ethical—but it carries a broad application, one that I have applied throughout my career as a wealth advisor.

My financial advisory career is largely one of dealing with perpetual efforts of self-deception. People *know* how markets perform over long periods of time, but sometimes they desperately want to believe that we can time the markets that they *will* themselves to believe that it is possible. People know that a 10 percent "safe and guaranteed" annual return from their friend's real estate developer contact is, well, not "safe and guaranteed." They just want so badly for it to be true that they will go to extraordinary lengths to convince themselves that it is.

These are not intellectual issues; they are behavioral. Our human nature wants certain things to be true, so much so that we adjust our beliefs to get to the conclusion we want. It is epistemological self-deception, and in my career, we call it the challenge of behavioral management.

For twenty-five years, one of my mentors, Nick Murray, has taught me about the realities of human nature in investing. One of the reasons his messages have resonated with me so deeply is that my father's own philosophical legacy was consistent with this understanding. I care about human emotions, inclinations, and frailties in investment decisions because they drive the outcomes I am duty-bound to help to succeed. I know these emotions, inclinations, and frailties are *not primarily cognitive*, and require something other than strictly logical argument.

As a professional wealth advisor, I have to have a philosophy of how markets work that leads to a strategy for portfolio construction. I also need to have a philosophy of how human beings behave and what that means for their financial well-being. These two things are separate but connected. A successful investment philosophy and the resulting strategy must be consistent with a reasonable philosophy of human nature and behavior. One without the other will prove insufficient if the goal is to connect a portfolio to the achievement of human goals.

TYING IT ALL TOGETHER

By understanding markets as the forum where humans act, create, and produce, I have come to believe in bottom-up human activity as the source of wealth. Also, by observing that human beings have a strong ability to convince themselves to believe false things that they want to be true, I have been driven to search for an investment strategy which accounts for this human frailty.

The consequent investment strategy is called dividend growth investing, born of The Bahnsen Group's philosophical commitments. What I hope to establish in subsequent chapters is that dividend growth is a logical, cogent, and optimal strategy given this philosophy. What I hope to establish is that dividend growth, when executed right, accounts for the nature of markets, the nature of human beings, and the nature of things.

To that end, we work.

CHAPTER TWO

THE THESIS RESTATED

"Dividends are like rewards for patience and loyalty, a tangible expression of a company's gratitude to its shareholders."

—Peter Lynch

I REMAIN SURPRISED, TWO AND a half decades into my professional investing career, that dividend growth is known, understood, and implemented by very few. Selfishly, this works out well for me: the more this approach to equity investing remains a niche, the better for me, I suppose. I say "surprised," though, because the itches it could scratch for accumulators and withdrawers, for the aggressive and the conservative, for the income objective and the "growth" objective, are so plentiful and so self-evident, it remains mystifying to me that this corner of the investing universe is so small.

Even if understanding of the dividend growth strategy were more widespread, *some* would still reject it. As I reference in the introduction to this book and expand on in Chapter Four, there is something *countercultural* about dividend growth investing. It is consciously *not* about gaming the system, which goes against the desire to believe that one's investment approach represents "an edge" that others do not have. Dividend growth investing asserts that management alignment with shareholders matters, when many investors don't want to believe that management or shareholders are pertinent to stock success at all. Between aspirational traders, momentum players, HODL (hold on for dear life) investors, and those who believe dividends are a sign of weakness in a company's growth strategy, our culture is full of people who would reject dividend growth investing on its own terms—some with more plausible explanations than others—even if they did understand it.

However, before we get to the errors of those consciously rejecting dividend growth investing who do have a proper understanding of what it is, let's address the far larger segment of the investment population that simply knows not what they reject.

WHAT IT'S NOT

Dividend growth investing is not a substitute for bond investing. It does generate income, and that income can be captured regularly and systematically for those wanting cash flow (much like bonds). However, the primary characteristics of the fixed income asset class are categorically different. Using a basic Treasury bond or high-grade corporate bond as an example of bond investing, we would likely describe the major characteristics as:

- A maturity date where principal is returned;
- Consistent cash flow that does not fluctuate; and
- Minimal volatility in the underlying price of the bond.

Dividend equity represents perpetual ownership that lacks the security (or insecurity) of a cash-in date. Its cash flow is not fixed but is intended to rise consistently over time. The volatility may be less than a broader index of stocks, but it is higher than a vanilla bond portfolio. In other words, dividend growth investing is zero for three in the three major characteristics people associate with bond investing.

Dividend growth investing is not a substitute for risk asset investing, either. It is a way to pursue risk premia. I believe it is an extremely reliable, rational, and rewarding one, but it is not a way to trade some return for higher assurances. Describing it as a way for stock investors to "win less but also lose less" is not quite accurate, theoretically or historically. That may have proven true at some point, but multiple chapters in this book will make the argument that the dividend growth investor is not giving up long-term rewards for the other benefits they gain. Rather, they are optimizing the social contract and incentive structure of their investment arrangement.

Dividend growth is not a way to sacrifice innovation and profit growth for boredom and mediocrity. If done right, it should be less exciting (yes, more boring) than some alternatives, but it should also be, across a properly constructed and well-diversified portfolio, filled with innovation, growth, and opportunity.

WHAT IT IS

Dividend growth investing is about the return of profits to the owners (risk-takers) of a business. Those owners are, in almost all cases I describe in this book, minority owners of a public company in which they have no operational control. (If you are reading this as a 51 percent owner of a public company with a C-suite position, forgive me). As Chapter Eight will exhaustively cover, dividend growth investing is not about what a company does to generate profits; it is about how management treats the profits that a successful business generates. A dividend growth company could be a cutting-edge technology company involved in transformative innovation or it could be a public utility that provides gas and electricity to Midwestern Americans. What makes the company a dividend growth company is that it (a) has profits, (b) has chosen to return a portion of those to its owners in the form of a dividend, and (c) has a profit profile and commitment/comfort/intention which enables it to grow that profit return year-over-year.

Can this be possible with a company that has wild profits one year on one deal or event (such as the approval of a miracle drug it has been working on for over a decade, with no other business lines at all), but no stability in the underlying business model? No, it cannot. So, the presupposition in the dividend growth universe is that a company is a consistent cash flow generator, and that its business model has a past, present, and future that will continue to generate profit. It is hard to be a company like that, but it sure is wonderful to be one!

But something is missing once a company has a strategy and business model that allows it to theoretically return profits (at a growing pace) to its owners each year: the commitment to actually doing so. There are plenty of companies whose management teams can do quite well for themselves not returning profits to the owners, instead utilizing stock buybacks (perfectly legal and moral), guidance gamesmanship (less moral and potentially less legal), or financial engineering (even less moral and legal). That is a wide array of options for the focus to be on stock price optics (not monolithic, and not suggestive that all such situations involve immorality or criminality), but the point is that the vast majority of public equity ownership lacks optimal incentives for alignment. Where that alignment exists, the dividend becomes a quasi-contractual obligation (not literally, but practically) that transcends the fakery and gamesmanship of stock price optics.

Dividend growth investing comes with a reward for past risk taken, paid from current success, but it carries a promise about the future, as well.

That last part is important. Dividend growth investing provides the benefit of receiving a dividend (which amortizes you every time you receive it—it de-risks the investor every quarter—since the principal-at-risk has been reduced), but it also involves the sign, confidence, and statement about the future that management is making.

Too many think that dividend growth investing is about them: "I don't need the dividend." "I am aggressive and young. I don't mind the company not returning profits to me at this stage." Those are not completely cogent thoughts in their own right, but even if they accurately capture the way some investors feel, they personalize dividend growth investing as if it were exclusively about them and miss what it means for the companies themselves.

Dividend growth investing is only a possibility to be bought, invested in, and utilized as a portfolio strategy where companies have consistent free cash flow. The ability to reliably sustain that dividend requires a prudent use of leverage. It forces management to invest company capital at a higher return on invested capital than its own cost of capital. And perhaps, most importantly, it constrains the ego to which all human beings are susceptible—yes, even the corporate managers you give your money to—to avoid the capital-destroying acquisitions that are driven more by empire-building than real value creation. It fosters prudent capital stewardship.

INVESTORS WHO ACCUMULATE

The thesis behind dividend growth investing is filled with claims about investors that really do matter. Investors benefitting from the auto-compounding of dividend reinvestment is not a small point—it is wealth-building at a mathematical force people can hardly comprehend, especially with the blessed miracle of market volatility over time (see Chapter Six). It is compounding the return of an underlying asset *along with* the additional shares that came from dividends. It is double compounding, a mathematical miracle inside a mathematical miracle. The fruit from the tree continues to grow, but the tree generating the fruit grows too, leading to even more fruit (dividends), and an even larger tree (portfolio base). This is a vital part of the case for dividend growth investing, and it is investor focused.

INVESTORS WHO SPEND

The withdrawal benefits of dividend growth investing are also investor focused and powerful. I put a real-life chart using real-life math in *The Case for Dividend Growth* that non-hypothetically showed someone with $2 million at the beginning of the new century, investing entirely in the S&P 500, withdrawing $120,000 per year for living expenses (it did not factor for taxes or inflation at all, which would have made things much worse), and ending the decade with $500,000.

Here, I offer the same chart, extended to show the additional returns after that horrific decade. What you see is that the market earned 5.33 percent per year over the fifteen years that the investor was withdrawing 6 percent per year of the initial capital. While that would still have led to a slight decline in principal, if just matching the delta between withdrawal and performance, what actually happened was that the investor ran out of money—a 100 percent evaporation of principal despite a positive (though subpar) return that was very close to the withdrawal rate of the initial balance. And worse, you'd see that with five more years, the portfolio actually performed at well more than double the amount of withdrawal (compounding at nearly 14 percent for the two decades put together. But alas, it is irrelevant, because the investor was down 75 percent after one decade, and out of money after fifteen years.

Chart: S&P 500 Investor Illustration—the Danger of Negative Compounding

			6% of starting value, every year	
YEAR	Beginning Value	Return	Withdrawal	Ending Balance
2000	$ 2,000,000	-9.10%	$ (120,000)	$ 1,708,920
2001	$ 1,708,920	-11.89%	$ (120,000)	$ 1,399,997
2002	$ 1,399,997	-22.10%	$ (120,000)	$ 997,118
2003	$ 997,118	28.68%	$ (120,000)	$ 1,128,675
2004	$ 1,128,675	10.88%	$ (120,000)	$ 1,118,419
2005	$ 1,118,419	4.91%	$ (120,000)	$ 1,047,442
2006	$ 1,047,442	15.79%	$ (120,000)	$ 1,073,885
2007	$ 1,073,885	5.49%	$ (120,000)	$ 1,006,253
2008	$ 1,006,253	-37.00%	$ (120,000)	$ 558,339
2009	$ 558,339	23.40%	$ (120,000)	**$ 540,911**
		0.91%	Average return, full decade	
2010	$ 540,911	15.10%	$ (120,000)	$ 484,468
2011	$ 484,468	2.10%	$ (120,000)	$ 372,122
2012	$ 372,122	16.00%	$ (120,000)	$ 292,462
2013	$ 292,462	32.40%	$ (120,000)	$ 228,339
2014	$ 228,339	13.70%	$ (120,000)	$ 123,182
2015	$ 123,182	1.40%	$ (120,000)	$ 3,226
		5.33%	Average return from start to finish	
2016	$ 3,226	11.96%	$ (120,000)	$ -
2017	$ -	21.83%	$ (120,000)	$ -
2018	$ -	-4.38%	$ (120,000)	$ -
2019	$ -	31.49%	$ (120,000)	$ -
2020	$ -	18.40%	$ (120,000)	$ -
		13.78%	Average return, second decade	

The simple math here is that withdrawals that are constant (people live and eat, and hence spend, every year) when returns are not (despite positive returns over time) create an effect called negative compounding. Negative compounding erodes wealth; in this case, the results were fatal.

Some may say, "Well, that 2000 to 2009 period will never happen again. Look at what has happened since!" Could it be that the 2010–2025 returns may not be repeatable? I think the future of profit growth and a market economy for investors is very bright, but if I had to pick between the likelihood of a repeat of a lost decade or a repeat of fifteen years that barely have a down year and compound over 16 percent per year, it would take me five seconds to cast my vote on a probability basis.

But I digress. The point here is not forecasting the future or even projecting the past onto the future. It is just doing math. A withdrawal strategy that only takes from that which is positive (dividends) and keeps the principal intact (despite its value fluctuation), is immunized from negative compounding. Here, we see the same dollar setup as the prior example ($2 million invested), where they will just take the dividends generated every year. The total return uses the actual return of the Dividend Aristocrat Index from 2000 to 2020, but that component is almost immaterial. In this hypothetical case, the investor earned the same total return as the other S&P 500 investor withdrawing $120,000 (13.8 percent for twenty calendar years). But with dividend growing at 6 percent per year (at the very, very low end of what we believe a proper dividend growth strategy should and would be over twenty years), the income received is double that of the other investor, and much more important, the value of the portfolio is intact. In fact, it is $300,000 higher than where it started despite $3.5 million being withdrawn over twenty years. The total economic gain is 3x that of the other scenario.

Chart: Dividend Growth Investor Illustration: The Benefits of Dividend Withdrawal

				Withdrawing the dividends every year	
YEAR	Beginning Value	Yield on Cost	Return	Withdrawal	Ending Balance
2000	$ 2,000,000	4.50%	10.10%	$ (90,000)	$ 2,102,910
2001	$ 2,102,910	4.77%	10.20%	$ (95,400)	$ 2,212,276
2002	$ 2,212,276	5.06%	-11.40%	$ (101,124)	$ 1,870,481
2003	$ 1,870,481	5.36%	26.10%	$ (107,191)	$ 2,223,508
2004	$ 2,223,508	5.68%	14.40%	$ (113,623)	$ 2,413,708
2005	$ 2,413,708	6.02%	3.76%	$ (120,440)	$ 2,379,495
2006	$ 2,379,495	6.38%	16.20%	$ (127,667)	$ 2,616,624
2007	$ 2,616,624	6.77%	-1.40%	$ (135,327)	$ 2,446,559
2008	$ 2,446,559	7.17%	-20.50%	$ (143,446)	$ 1,830,975
2009	$ 1,830,975	7.60%	23.30%	$ (152,053)	**$ 2,070,111**
			7.08%	Average return, full decade	
2010	$ 2,070,111	7.98%	19.23%	$ (159,656)	$ 2,277,835
2011	$ 2,277,835	8.46%	8.40%	$ (169,235)	$ 2,285,722
2012	$ 2,285,722	8.97%	16.20%	$ (179,389)	$ 2,447,559
2013	$ 2,447,559	9.51%	31.52%	$ (190,153)	$ 2,968,941
2014	$ 2,968,941	10.08%	14.20%	$ (201,562)	$ 3,160,347
2015	$ 3,160,347	10.68%	0.80%	$ (213,655)	**$ 2,970,266**
			9.89%	Average return until 2015	
2016	$ 2,970,266	11.32%	11.20%	$ (226,475)	$ 3,051,095
2017	$ 3,051,095	12.00%	20.50%	$ (240,063)	$ 3,387,294
2018	$ 3,387,294	12.72%	-3.10%	$ (254,467)	$ 3,035,709
2019	$ 3,035,709	13.49%	27.90%	$ (269,735)	$ 3,537,681
2020	$ 3,537,681	14.30%	9.20%	$ (285,919)	**$ 3,550,924**
			13.83%	Average return, second decade	
				$ 3,576,581	**Withrawals taken**
				$ 2,289,615	**Balance in 2020**
				$ 5,866,196	**Value to investor**

I have to reiterate—the "annual returns" are the same here—that the results to the investors couldn't be more different. The difference is almost entirely related to the withdrawal mechanics—enjoying a growing income that doesn't invade principal, versus withdrawing from principal and counting on price appreciation as a substitute for income in a period when prices are depreciating. It is all just math, but in this case, it is also history.

Speaking of which, the history I highlighted here is the past twenty to twenty-five years of investing history, as it is the most familiar and tangible. It also contains some extremes that should counter the idea that some investing truisms are not ever-present realities. No one can say, "Sure, the 2000 to 2008 period was bad, but normally you get a better recovery than that!" because the past seventeen years have been the best recovery markets have ever seen. Yet, I am sure there are some who may say, "Well, that 2000 to 2009 flat market is ahistorical, and represents an anomaly." Of course, the 1966–1981 period is even longer, and though, *with dividends,* the returns were nominally positive (+1.8 percent per year for fifteen years), the real return was substantially negative (I can only be nice in all this data by ignoring inflation for so long). Even the nominally positive return required dividends to be so, and the volatility along the way exacerbated the danger of linear withdrawals of capital even more than the 2000–2008 period.

History is filled with these periods, and I am unwilling to assume that the future will not contain at least some form of multi-year range-bound markets.

COMPANIES THAT DO THIS

If I were forced to focus on one benefit of dividend growth investing, as many as there are, it would not be either of the two "investor benefits" I just highlighted. It would not be the accumulation mechanics or the withdrawal protection, as much as I prize both. It would be what it means about the *companies* more than the *investors.*

The major thesis behind dividend growth investing is that the corporate disciplines that enable it offer extraordinary protection from risk and align investors with the best side of business performance and acumen. It allows investor return to come from that dynamic I described in Chapter One: the creative, productive, innovative aspect of human action. It requires much less of the return to be about investor sentiment and instead makes the source of the return the business endeavor itself. Put differently, dividends are endogenous (created by the business itself), and what many investors are relying on is exogenous (a by-product of the psychology of the masses).

I believe that dividend growth and the corporate culture that fosters it exists when management views their shareholders as fellow owners of the business (which they are), and not as speculators and traders renting shares and happy to go along with whatever stock price optics might work.

CONCLUSION

When I describe *investor* benefits and *company* benefits as fundamental to the dividend growth thesis, I am not establishing an *either/or* binary; I am highlighting a *both/and* scenario. I believe the portfolio math investors benefit from (the arguments I learned from Lowell Miller) and the corporate behavior investors benefit from (the arguments I learned from Daniel Peris) are not at all mutually exclusive.

Companies do not deliver capital gains. Now, of course, we understand finance economics well enough to know that, in theory, companies that grow earnings and create value should see their enterprise value grow (capital appreciation).

But it is not that simple, as many companies grow earnings yet suffer declining share prices, and many companies lose money but see escalating share prices. The market votes on how to price those shares based on sentiment, psychology, hype, and emotion, all the time. Dividend growth investors only receive dividends from the performance of a company—those human endeavors that drive profitable and productive activity at scale. Capital appreciation is inseparable from the sentiment of a crowd and is not directly about the performance of a business.

That is the thesis behind dividend growth investing. It is about investors seeing themselves as minority owners of a business—a good and profitable business—where management also sees them as owners. It is about companies that optimize their risk management and growth initiatives to an unwritten contract to reliably meet this dividend growth expectation.

And then, it becomes about this superior alignment and business performance translating into tangible benefits to these business owners, who reap the benefits of growing cash flows and true wealth creation.

CHAPTER THREE

THE TESTIMONY OF HISTORY

"Over the past 81 years, then, reinvested dividend income accounted for approximately 95% of the compound long-term return earned by the companies in the S&P 500. In other words, the reinvestment of dividends accounted for almost all of stocks' long-term total return."

—JOHN BOGLE

IT WOULD BE NEWS TO most investors of this era that dividends have historically accounted for a significant portion of investor returns. Indeed, John Bogle's quotation above would seem unfathomable to most investors, first because eighty-one years is just too long of a timeline to seem relevant, but also because the secret sauce of that 95 percent math is in the reinvestment of the dividends. Yet, even without the compounding magic of reinvestment, the S&P 500, despite its low yield,[1] has gotten 37 percent of its return from dividends over the past century. And with the magic of compounding (or you can just say the math of compounding), the contribution of reinvested dividends is striking!

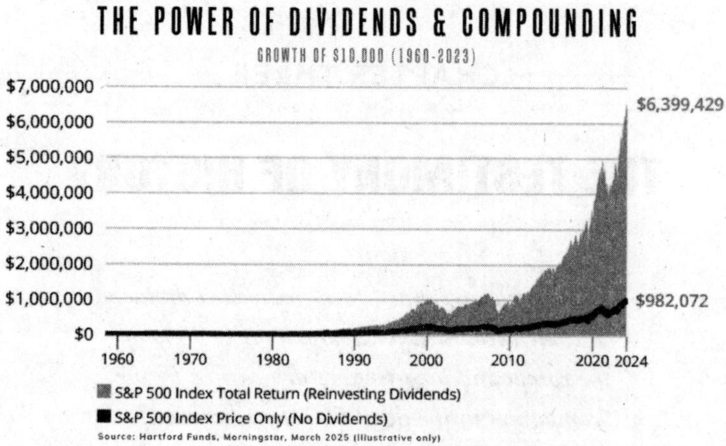

SHOULD WE CARE?

Those who began their investing life on this side of the Global Financial Crisis of 2008 have had very little reason to consider dividends. The S&P 500 has compounded at an annual growth rate of 15 percent since 2009, when the market began its post-crisis recovery. Over that time period, the yield of the S&P was between 1.1 percent and 2.5 percent nearly the entire time, meaning that investors felt they could ignore

1 As of the date of this writing, the current yield of the S&P 500 is 1.15 percent.

it (a small bit of icing on the cake of a much larger return). Additionally, it is hardly a subject the media likes to cover, as the hype and excitement of markets is not as attached to a 1.5 percent dividend yield. What makes for clicks and ratings are big price moves (up or down, it doesn't matter which), and the media excels in that which is sensationalistic, not that which seems boring or mechanical.

The fact of the matter is that even for the S&P 500, dividends have mattered a great deal throughout history, despite what those with very short-term memory banks might say. Yes, in very strong decades of price return, they matter less mathematically (1990s, 2010s), but from 2000 to 2009 they were *over 100 percent of the total return* (since the index had a negative total return).

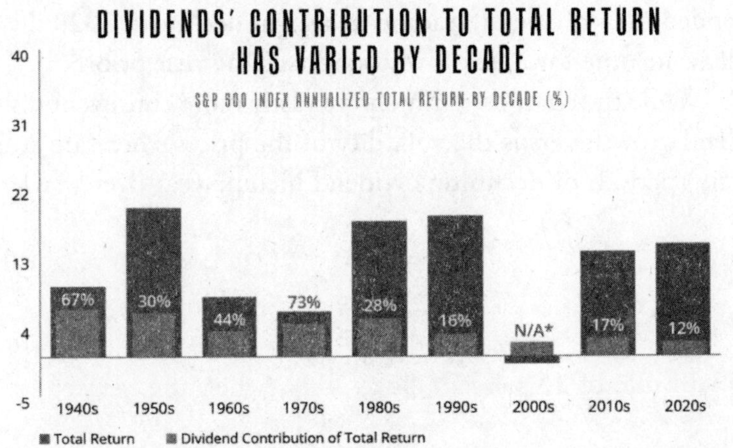

As of 12/31/24. **Past performance does not guarantee future results.** Indices are unmanaged and not available for direct investment. *Total return for the S&P 500 index was negative for the 2000s. Dividends provided a 1.8% annualized return over the decade. For illustrative purposes only. Data Sources: Morningstar and Hartford Funds, 3/25.

DIVIDENDS IN TIMES OF TROUBLE

What I find most fascinating, though, is how even the S&P 500 dividends have stayed so reliable over the years, despite a large portion of the index not committed to dividends at all, let alone dividend growth.

In the bear market of 1973 and 1974, the S&P 500 declined 48 percent in price. Its underlying earnings declined 18 percent. The dividends were not down at all, though. In the 2000–2002 bear market, the S&P 500 declined 49 percent, the underlying earnings were down 30 percent, and yet the dividends were only down 6 percent. The financial crisis decline saw the S&P 500 drop 57 percent, with underlying earnings down 32 percent, and the dividends down 20 percent. In the COVID-19 year of 2020, despite a positive price performance from the index, forty-four companies cut or suspended their dividend, leading to a slight decline in 2020 dividend income for index investors versus the year prior.[2]

While the chart certainly shows vastly more consistent dividend growth versus the volatility of the prices, there are still (rare) periods of declining dividend income year-over-year.

2 Howard Silverblatt, Senior Index Analyst, S&P Dow Jones Indices, https://www.indexologyblog.com/author/howard_silverblatt/.

S&P 500 INDEX & DIVIDENDS

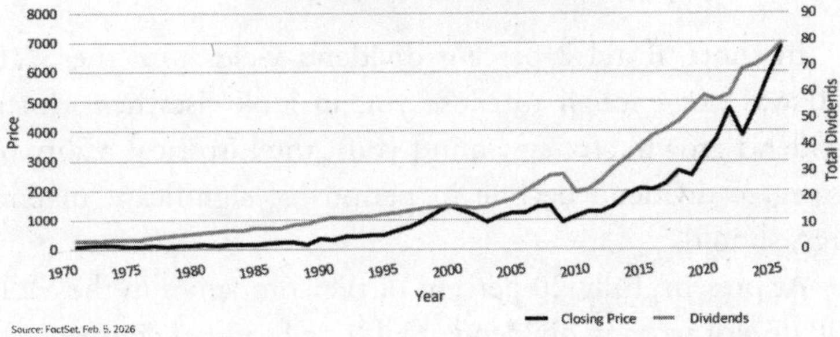

DIVIDEND GROWTH INVESTORS CAN DO BETTER

All at once, you see two things in these historical stress tests about the dividends of the S&P 500:

1. The dividends generally represent far more stability within the index than the prices, and even the underlying earnings (largely because of the moderate dividend payout ratio of many companies, giving them flexibility to maintain the dividend during tough times).

And yet:

2. As opposed to a portfolio strategy exclusively focused on dividend growth companies, the S&P 500 has not been a perfectly reliable solution for year-over-year consistency and growth of dividends. A 20 percent decline in the financial crisis is much less than the price return decline of 57 percent, but it confounds the idea

of reliable, impenetrable dividend growth that is actually available to investors

In short, if a 1.2 percent dividend yield from the S&P 500 was not enough to cause you to look elsewhere (for a dividend growth strategy, mind you), the historical reality of aggregate dividend decline in periods of significant market stress should.

At present, fully 20 percent of the companies in the S&P 500 do not pay any dividend at all (one hundred companies). More than 60 percent of the index constituents pay a small or insignificant dividend. Only 36 percent of the S&P 500 companies can be counted on to grow the dividend each year. Less than 20 percent of the S&P 500 constituents offer a dividend yield above 2.5 percent, and not all of them are consistent dividend growers.

In short, the index is not a place for attractive dividend income or reliable dividend growth—and this is by design.

Yet, even *that* index powerfully reinforces the historical value of dividends and the superior reliability of dividends relative to the price return and earnings growth of the broader market.

Anecdotally, a focus on companies that are in a position to grow their dividend year-over-year shows charts that look like this:

PROCTER & GAMBLE CO. (PG)

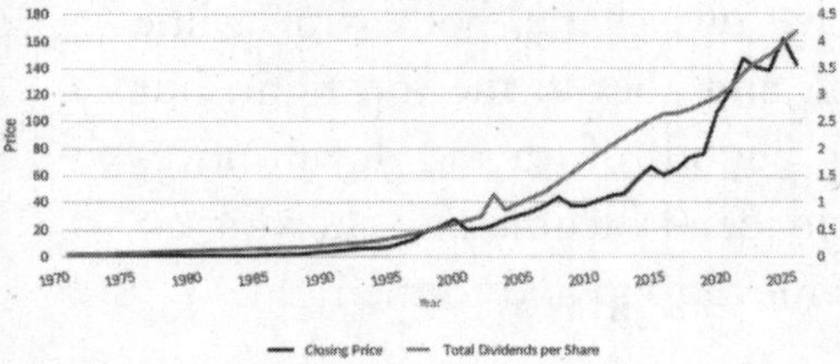

Year	Total Dividends Per Share	Year	Total Dividends Per Share
1970	0.04	1998	0.54
1971	0.05	1999	0.61
1972	0.05	2000	0.67
1973	0.05	2001	0.73
1974	0.06	2002[*]	1.14
1975	0.06	2003	0.87
1976	0.07	2004	0.98
1977	0.08	2005	1.09
1978	0.09	2006	1.21
1979	0.10	2007	1.96
1980	0.11	2008	1.55
1981	0.12	2009	1.72
1982	0.13	2010	1.99
1983	0.13	2011	2.06
1984	0.16	2012	2.21
1985	0.16	2013	2.37
1986	0.17	2014	2.53
1987	0.17	2015	2.63
1988	0.18	2016	2.67
1989	0.21	2017	2.74
1990	0.25	2018	2.84
1991	0.25	2019	2.96
1992	0.27	2020	3.12
1993	0.29	2021	3.40
1994	0.33	2022	3.61
1995	0.38	2023	3.74
1996	0.43	2024	3.96
1997	0.48	2025	4.18

[*] Spike for 2002 due to special disposition dividend because of the Jif and Crisco spinoff and merging with the J.M. Smucker Company on May 31, 2002.

Note: Data is from Yahoo Finance for chart and tables.
https://finance.yahoo.com/quote/PG/history/

CHEVRON CORP (CVX)

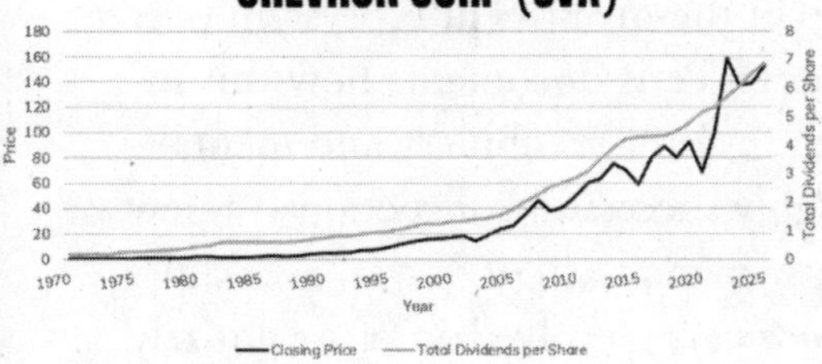

Year	Total Dividends Per Share	Year	Total Dividends Per Share
1970	0.2	1998	1.2
1971	0.2	1999	1.2
1972	0.2	2000	1.3
1973	0.2	2001	1.3
1974	0.2	2002	1.4
1975	0.3	2003	1.4
1976	0.3	2004	1.5
1977	0.3	2005	1.8
1978	0.3	2006	2.0
1979	0.4	2007	2.3
1980	0.5	2008	2.5
1981	0.5	2009	2.7
1982	0.6	2010	2.8
1983	0.6	2011	3.1
1984	0.6	2012	3.5
1985	0.6	2013	3.9
1986	0.6	2014	4.2
1987	0.6	2015	4.3
1988	0.6	2016	4.3
1989	0.7	2017	4.3
1990	0.7	2018	4.5
1991	0.8	2019	4.8
1992	0.8	2020	5.2
1993	0.9	2021	5.3
1994	0.9	2022	5.7
1995	1.0	2023	6.0
1996	1.0	2024	6.5
1997	1.1	2025	6.8

Note: Data is from Yahoo Finance and Chevron for chart and tables.
https://finance.yahoo.com/quote/CVX/history/
https://chevroncorp.gcs-web.com/unocal-archive

JOHNSON & JOHNSON (JNJ)

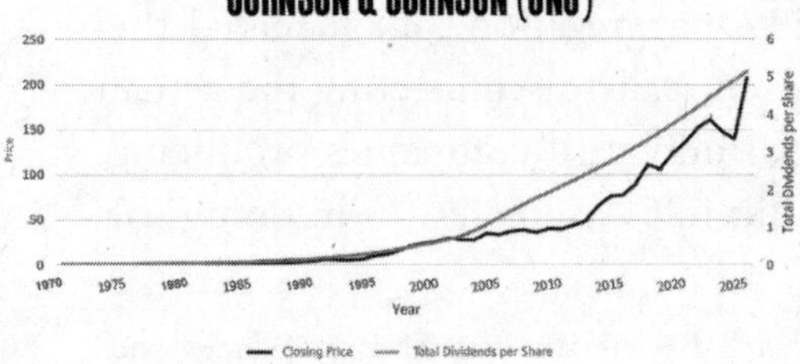

Year	Total Dividends Per Share	Year	Total Dividends Per Share
1970	0.01	1998	0.48
1971	0.01	1999	0.55
1972	0.01	2000	0.62
1973	0.01	2001	0.70
1974	0.02	2002	0.80
1975	0.02	2003	0.93
1976	0.02	2004	1.10
1977	0.03	2005	1.29
1978	0.04	2006	1.45
1979	0.04	2007	1.62
1980	0.05	2008	1.60
1981	0.05	2009	1.93
1982	0.06	2010	2.11
1983	0.07	2011	2.25
1984	0.07	2012	2.40
1985	0.08	2013	2.59
1986	0.09	2014	2.75
1987	0.10	2015	2.95
1988	0.12	2016	3.15
1989	0.14	2017	3.32
1990	0.16	2018	3.54
1991	0.19	2019	3.75
1992	0.22	2020	3.98
1993	0.25	2021	4.19
1994	0.28	2022	4.45
1995	0.32	2023	4.70
1996	0.37	2024	4.91
1997	0.43	2025	5.14

Note: Data is from Yahoo Finance for chart and tables.
https://finance.yahoo.com/quote/JNJ/history/

You will note that while they are not immune to stock price volatility, the dividends are. A diversified portfolio of dividend growers should have two charts, both with a line that starts at the bottom left and goes to the top right, but with the price level showing periods of up and down movement on the way, and the dividend income line showing an uninterrupted diagonal line moving up and to the right.

EYE OFF THE BALL

Understanding the origin of declining investor focus on dividends requires us to understand the history of the S&P 500 index, and its evolving role in the investment ecosystem over the last several decades. Daniel Peris documents how this index evolution changed both investor vocabulary and mentality.[3] The S&P 500 was a highly successful concoction—a new and improved way to *measure* market activity—yet, over time, Peris notes, a changing *vocabulary* evolved into an entirely different *mentality*. The aggregate metrics of the index began being referred to as a source of underlying corporate activity. "The index grew earnings by XYZ percent" is an incoherent statement, since an index does not have earnings, let alone growth of earnings. Of course, we all know what was and is meant by such convenience aggregation, but it served the purpose over many decades of really disconnecting the actual function of a stock market (individual companies producing goods and services and achieving various results in doing so)

3 Daniel Peris, "Dr. Frankenstein's Benchmark: The S&P 500 Index and the Observer Paradox," *American Affairs* IX, no. 3 (2025) https://americanaffairsjournal.org/2025/08/dr-frankensteins-benchmark-the-sp-500-index-and-the-observer-paradox/.

with the way investors think about it (now a faceless, nameless, company-less, amorphous "thing" that could be bought as an investment in and of itself). Peris points out that in the aftermath of the explosion of index popularity, further carve-outs took place that served the purpose of additionally disconnecting the investor from the underlying companies involved (such as FAANG and the Magnificent Seven).

In short, the S&P 500 was an index created to *measure* the market, and it has become an investment product that *moves* the market. And, for Peris, that means that the S&P 500 has become *a quasi-momentum product.*

DISTORTION OF MODERN ORTHODOXY

The relevance of all this to how investors used to think about dividends and how they think about them now is profound. But it does not start nor end with dividends. The massive concentration of a few key names in a capitalization-weighted index like the S&P 500 has changed the game (in keeping with the "momentum, not measurement" thesis of the index). The index's composition now having single stocks represent north of 7 percent of the 500-stock portfolio, or a basket of five to ten stocks equal 40 percent of the weighting, has fundamentally changed functionality. The entire Capital Asset Pricing Model (CAPM) was invented to measure the expected rate of return for an asset by analyzing its risk relative to the whole market, and consequently the excess return one would need to compensate for the risk being taken. To call it revolutionary in modern finance would be like calling Newtonian physics revolutionary in science—it understates the gravity of the moment. (See what I did there?) A key ingredient in

CAPM is Beta, the sensitivity of an asset's return to the overall market. The entire use of CAPM and Beta since the 1960s is based on measuring a stock's sensitivity to market movement—but now, it is the market that is sensitive to the movement of a few mega-cap stock names, not vice versa. The causation in CAPM has been reversed, or at least distorted, leading to formulas that no longer work as intended, but serve as the basis of most asset allocation models across the institutional investing world.

MOMENTUM VERSUS CASH FLOW

The enormous success of the S&P 500 in moving from a *measurement* to a *product* has (unintentionally) served the purpose of investors thinking about something called a "market," and various "factors" that temporarily move this market in various seasons, as opposed to "companies" that grow "profits." Dividend growth investing is about particular companies with particular business models that either succeed or fail, that either execute well or do not, that are intended to result in (a) the creation of profits, and (b) a distribution of some of those profits to the underlying owners of those businesses. When investor vocabulary and mentality shifts from something company-centric to something market-centric, it is entirely understandable why interest in dividends would get lost in the shuffle. Unbeknownst to a generation of investors, they have become momentum-factor investors (which has done well, at least for the past seventeen years) as opposed to the traditional concern of, well, receiving profits from the businesses in which one is invested.

HISTORY OR A NEW NORMAL?

Some will say that, historically, fewer growth opportunities existed for companies to redeploy profits into, so returning capital to shareholders made more sense; however, *now* it is different! *Now,* companies have greater opportunity to use mergers and acquisitions (M&A), financial engineering, global expansion, and technology investment as a way of profitably reallocating capital in a better way than investors can. During the 1990s, paying a dividend became, for some, an admission that management lacked an adequate "growth at all cost" focus. This became a bug, not a feature.

Historically, focus on core competency, being constrained by a dividend payout policy, and managing the reinvestment of profits into suitable growth initiatives in a manner governed by *prudence* and *shareholder alignment* were cultural expectations. At some point, for many, the boom success of the technology-and-growth craze in the 1990s meant the rules were different, and that if management didn't have an idea for reinvesting that capital versus returning it to shareholders, they better come up with one!

As my prior chapter indicated, I believe in two categories of argument for the dividend growth approach: investor-centric arguments and company-centric arguments. It is imperative to note within the (flawed) "new normal" argument that there is not even an attempt to argue that things have changed for investors. That a significant amount of investors need periodic cash flow from their investments has not changed. That the majority of institutions have liabilities that match to assets has not changed (pension funds, endowments, foundations, and insurance companies). On this front, many just argue that "unrealized gains are the same as income," and it is my belief that this is one of the most dangerous assertions in all of investing, first for its obvious inaccuracy, and second for what happens when that inaccuracy gets established.

But even apart from the evergreen truth that investors invest for a return of cash as was the case for decade upon decade before indexing, momentum, and high-growth technology culture subverted investors psychology about dividends, the company-centric thesis has not changed whatsoever. It is simply untrue that corporate managers have become better allocators to new growth initiatives than they were in the prior century. People can always focus on exceptions, or those cases where reinvestment carries a high internal rate of return. Certain technology and platform businesses have enjoyed this dynamic—at least until they haven't (it can't last forever). Some technology companies thought and behaved this way successfully but then evolved into highly profitable companies with a high return of profits to investors, all the while retaining adequate profits for attractive reinvestment opportunity (such as Cisco, Texas Instruments, IBM, and Qualcomm). Far too many to count trafficked off of their rising stock price while boldly asserting they knew best when it came to what to do with profits before eventually crashing and burning (the dot-com names we can all recall, and other major players like Yahoo, Nokia, Blackberry, GoPro, Sun Microsystems, EMC, Zoom, Snapchat…I could go on and on). And, of course, other names have not converted to robust dividend payers but have done just fine with a massive moat around a massive business that has scaled better than almost any business in history (Apple, Google, Microsoft, and Meta).

The cultural shift in corporate America is not one where "all companies become like Apple and Microsoft." As best I can tell, Apple and Microsoft are going to have a hard time being like Apple and Microsoft going forward (the price of success), and those who dared to adopt their capital allocation attitude without their unique business features are either out of business or slowly dying. It is a feature of the US economy that investors have stood up exceptions to the rule like Meta, but they did not do it without investor mistakes like Twitter and Snapchat. Google belongs in the history books, but the footnotes in those books will have to mention the dozen companies that did not replicate its success.

In short, the primary theme of history remains the primary theme now—that companies who prioritize a return of profits to shareholders are companies who maintain durability, who manage risk, and who are most likely to succeed for the long haul. There are companies that fail with good capital return policies, sure, but this is the key: They did not fail because of their capital return policies. They failed because of something inherent in the business model or execution. The same cannot be said for most companies that fail with no capital return to shareholders. They either fail because they never did convert their hype into profitability (Problem 1), or they fail because they never converted their profitability into something sustainable (Problem 2). Their arrogant claims of "infinite growth opportunities" facilitated capital destruction as expensive M&A was pursued, noneconomic interests were prioritized, and vanity projects and non-core competencies destroyed the good things that the company was otherwise doing. This is perhaps the most consistent pattern in American corporate history.

CONCLUSION

One thing has served as the best antidote to it for decades upon decades. It has not been perfect, and has not been without exceptions and troubles along the way. But both theoretically and empirically, a responsible policy of dividend growth has rewarded shareholders, maintained access to capital markets for growth opportunity, created the right relationship between a company's cost of capital and desired return on invested capital, and produced the staying power that is a *sine qua non* for investor success.

CHAPTER FOUR

A NEEDED COUNTERCULTURAL MESSAGE

"To the extent we have been successful, it is because we concentrated on identifying one-foot hurdles that we could step over rather than because we acquired any ability to clear seven-footers."

—Warren Buffett

"The investor's chief problem—and even his worst enemy—is likely to be himself."

—Benjamin Graham

THE COUNTERCULTURAL MESSAGE OF DIVIDEND growth investing has nothing to do with technology, growth, and innovation, as if the culture celebrates those things while dividend growth investing rejects them. There is nothing inconsistent with dividend growth investing and technology, growth, and innovation. The need for a countercultural impulse in embracing dividend growth investing comes from the culture's love affair with *huge, quick returns* that human nature desperately wants to believe can be infinitely found and constantly repeated.

BELIEVING IN MAKE-BELIEVE

Being countercultural does not mean being anti-technology. It means being anti-wishful thinking. It means believing that risk management matters. It means that history has lessons to teach us. It means understanding the basic grown-up reality that big gains that come easily can be lost easily. It means seeing the world for how it is and not how we want it to be.

A society that believes unbelievable things is going to invest in unsustainable ways. The dividend growth investor is countercultural because the dividend growth investor must be willing to cut against the grain of cultural orthodoxies that are not rooted in reality.

The belief that expensive stocks will only get more expensive may very well work out, at least for a period. It generally requires some prescience about what will prove successful (fair enough), and it also requires some good fortune in timing one's exit. But the cultural norm is to believe that what has done abundantly well, above and beyond historical averages, will continue doing just that. History has not been kind to this mentality or practice.

HISTORY IN PRACTICE

On the day this chapter was written, Nvidia (NVDA) was trading at a share price of $188. It had been $12 just three and a half years before. A stock going up 15x in a few years is a pretty good portfolio result. Where it will go by the time you are reading this is unknown to me, and immaterial. No matter what happens from here on, what has already happened for Nvidia is something that many investors envy.

NVIDIA CORPORATION (NVDA-USA) **02/05/2021 - 02/06/2026**

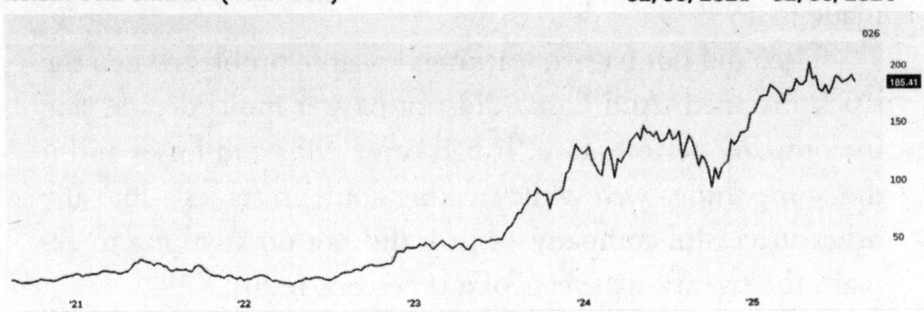

Source: NVIDIA Corporation, 02/06/2026

But history says sometimes those charts do change, even for really good and dominant companies.

CISCO SYSTEMS, INC. (CSCO-USA) **02/16/1990 - 02/06/2026**

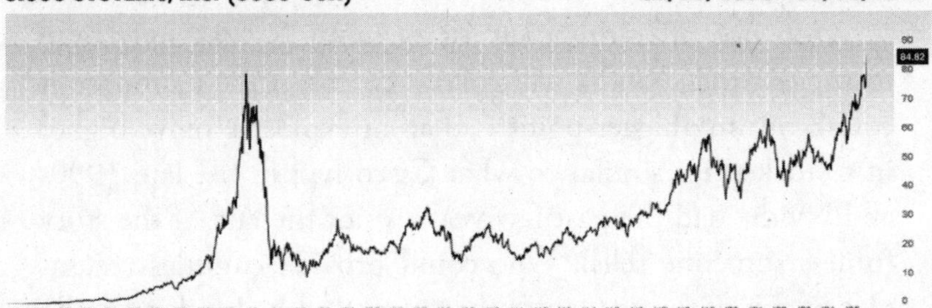

Source: Cisco Systems, Inc. 02/06/2026

What is most striking about Cisco's drop from $86 in 1999 to $10 in 2002 was that Cisco earned $3.7 billion in that three-year period. Yes, the company took some restructuring charges along the way (baked into that $3.7 billion figure) and the dot-com implosion led to some one-time excess inventory write-downs, but the company was heralded as the internet leader for its router and network and server business, and that would prove even more true than had been expected. Yet, the stock was down 88 percent. By the end of 2019, Cisco was at $39 per share, less than half of its 1999 high. It made $11.6 billion of profits in 2019, more than 5x what it made in 1999.

Cisco did not have an earnings collapse problem when the stock dropped. And Cisco did not have a multi-decade slog in company performance. It had some wins and losses and it did some things well while making some mistakes—like any other successful company—but it did not do anything to explain the twenty-five years of a 0 percent return.

Of course, investors who got in *after* the late-'90s bubble burst did not make 0 percent. The stock price compounded at about 9 percent per year since the 2002 bottom, and beginning in 2011, the company became a powerful dividend payer and grower, as well (a 12.5 percent compound annual growth rate [CAGR] since 2011).

I do not offer this contrast between Nvidia and Cisco to suggest that Nvidia will follow Cisco's path. I suppose it could, but my bigger point is that an explosive move higher in a stock price similar to what Cisco had in the late 1990s and Nvidia had the past few years is not the end of the story (unless someone sells). One could provide countless examples of this with companies that proved to be fundamentally broken, but I use Cisco as my generational example because it is hard to find a more successful company within the context of its space and industry. Investors are not used to thinking of generational success stories compounding at 0 percent for twenty-five years, but it happens when a stock price gets too far ahead of itself.

Microsoft is perhaps the most successful company in history, or at least on the Mount Rushmore of such. Its stock price was $58 at its 1999 high. Its stock was $58 at its 2016 high. A seventeen-year period of a 0 percent return, from a company with a 70 percent global market share of operating systems. Yes, the stock has exploded since 2016 as Microsoft reorganized its revenue model to something more subscription-oriented, and, even more importantly, added to its bundled enterprise stack powerful tools in cloud platforms. No one can deny the success of this reinvention, or the lifetime success of Microsoft, but a seventeen-year period of a flat return originating from an excessive valuation cannot be ignored, either.

RULES THAT DON'T ACTUALLY EVER CHANGE

There is nothing new under the sun, of course. Each period of robust "quick returns" was accompanied by declarations that everything was now permanently new. In fact, I read an article in 2025, as the promise of artificial intelligence (AI) was creating triple-digit percentage stock gains, that contained the line: "... this was a new economic era, to which old economic precedent no longer applied." That proclamation, however, was not written last year. It stems from a *New York Times* article titled "Some Popular Theories Which Prevailed in 1929,

And How They Were Tested by Events of the Autumn"—published on December 31, 1929.

Every mania in history has been accompanied by scoldings of doubters and skeptics. Whether it be mass media, Wall Street analysts, or company cheerleaders themselves, associating an unsustainable period with new rules of science, logic, and math creates a non-falsifiable argument. You cannot argue against the absurdities of excess if "all the old rules are out." It is not an effective argument as much as it is a way of making sure there will not be a reasoned argument at all.

The language of "new economy" and "new rules" and "new paradigms" is, well, not new. I suggest that one of the surest indicators that a hard lesson from history is about to surface, is when "promoters" begin vocalizing that history no longer has lessons to offer. Sometimes it is not just history that has lost its voice, but math, itself. Consider Scott McNealy's famous reminder about the math of his stock (Sun Microsystems) at its peak:

> At 10 times revenues, to give you a 10-year payback, I have to pay you 100% of revenues for 10 straight years in dividends. That assumes I can get that by my shareholders. That assumes I have zero cost of goods sold, which is very hard for a computer company. That assumes zero expenses, which is really hard with 39,000 employees. That assumes I pay no taxes, which is very hard. And that assumes you pay no taxes on your dividends, which is kind of illegal. And that assumes with zero R&D for the next 10 years, I can maintain the current revenue run rate. Now, having done that, would any of you like to buy my stock at $64?

> Do you realize how ridiculous those basic assumptions are? You don't need any transparency. You don't need any footnotes. What were you thinking?[1]

McNealy said this two years after the tech boom implosion, but he referenced a very important part of investing: math. Dividend growth investors seek to operate within a construct that is informed by math, logic, history, and economics.

And yes, that has become *countercultural.*

NUMBED BY ALL THE GOODNESS

We are living in a period of what feels like uninterrupted gains that has skewed withdrawal math reality for many investors. Even if you just discard the idea of a market collapse or standard bear market, a (historically common) period of a flat, range-bound return would do extraordinary damage to those withdrawing from portfolios they believe will go up over 10 percent per year for years on end.

In the year 2020, the entire US economy shut down. A global pandemic came that was more severe than anything seen since 1918. Unemployment spiked higher. Schools, restaurants, and public places closed down for months on end (for far too long, but I digress). And what did the S&P 500 do that year? It increased by 16 percent. The 2009–2025 period for the market saw one down year in 2018 (barely down a meager 4.3 percent) and just one substantive down year

1 Hunter Lewis LLC, "Bubble Trouble," from a March 31, 2002, interview with Scott McNealy, https://www.hunterlewisllc.com/insights/bubble-trouble-dot-com-bubble.

in 2022 (a more meaningful decline of 18 percent). Fifteen of seventeen years have been positive, the compound annual growth rate is above 15 percent per year, and just since 2019 the index has *almost* tripled in value (from 2,500 to 7,000 on a price return basis).

Well, maybe this is all going to continue as it has been. I don't happen to believe it is, but I certainly acknowledge that these price returns and the factors behind them have defied the imagination. But my point is very simple: Much of the same rhetoric, sentiment, and expectation that has driven various mania excesses for time eternal can be found now. Each period of time where excess had to be repriced was preceded by excess apologists insisting that "this time was different."

What I do not want to suggest is that investors are wrong to enjoy the period they have been living in. Whether it is Nvidia's 100 percent return per year for the past three years, or the S&P 500 almost tripling over the past seven years, investors who have participated have every right to enjoy it. What I want to suggest, though, is that the laws of the universe have not been replaced. The current cultural moment screams that there will be more of the same. It advocates discarding valuations and reasonable forms of inquiry. It condones irrationality if irrationality aligns with what we want to be true. It tells you dramatic things can happen quickly and easily. The culture asks you to ignore the symmetry between risk and reward.

ARTIFICIAL INTELLIGENCE AND NATURAL SKEPTICISM

What about this AI moment? What about the idea that if we abandon certain ideas about cash flow, profits, dividends, management alignment, and various other norms and fundamentals, we can participate in a new revolution that will transcend the countercultural ethos I am advocating?

It is challenging to write about AI eight months before the book will come out. With the volatility that space has had, it is entirely possible a huge new rally will take place between now and then, and it is entirely possible that there will be a dramatic repricing between now and then. Of course, any number of things could happen in the AI and AI-adjacent sector between now and the publication of this book, and the unpredictability of those things is sort of my point.

The easy answer to the question "will a new sector revolution replace the laws of risk, math, logic, and economics?" is "no." I am not going to make the case that AI, as a space, faces a certain reckoning. Yes, capital expenditures seem way higher than a level that can be reconciled to future returns. Legitimate questions exist about the funding model, about competition from China, about the path to monetization, about the political and societal appetite for the sector's demands, and about so much more. I do suspect that the space will end up producing big winners (eventually), but also some noteworthy losers. I also believe that the role AI plays in commercial society over time is unknown right now, and that there will be substantial changes, pivots, and misunderstandings along the way to getting clarity on that issue.

But for our purposes, construct any view on the future of AI that you would like—nothing changes the fact that there will either be companies that generate profits from it, or there will not. To the extent that the hyper-scalers and infrastructure companies associated with the space, not to mention those who own and create the large language models, end up achieving profitability, they cannot do so if the consumers and businesses of the real economy are not using it to a productive end. The winners of the industrial revolution were not just the companies that made industrial machinery, but also those who used industrial machinery, and even those who benefited from its role in production. The digital revolution created profits for a plethora of software and hardware companies (and it also created more than a few bankrupt companies if we want to be honest about history), but its major gains were for everyone. It created an enhanced productivity and operational efficiency that boosted profits across defense and aerospace, biotech, consumer staples, and energy companies. That is sort of the point about anything "transformational"—the benefits are deep and wide, and not limited to those selling the thing that is transformational.

I see great upside for a diversified portfolio of dividend growth companies if AI exceeds societal expectations. I see something fatal for the stocks of many AI companies if it does not. The risk/reward skew here is not close. Investors who maintain a rational belief in discipline, profitability, a path to ROI, and other basic ingredients of prudent capital allocation will not be left in the dust. Those who don't, might be.

WHAT MATTERS LEAST IS WHAT THE DISTRACTION IS

Whether the subject at hand is the Nasdaq, the FAANG stocks, the Mag 7 stocks, AI stocks, or whatever else comes next, is irrelevant. In fact, it is far too limiting for me to reduce my examples here to various nomenclatures of groupings that all correlate to the technology sector (many of which have been very successful). The "thing" pulling investors off the sensible path could be cryptocurrencies, condos in Florida, oil and gas partnerships, or your Uber driver's friend's new hedge fund. Obviously these things are not all the same—some are credible investment solutions and some are scams. Some have a track record and some have a salesman. But what I refer to here is the belief that there is *something* out there that can permanently transcend the time-tested understanding and mechanics of dividend growth investing—because it is new, fresh, and exciting. The countercultural part of dividend growth investing is not that it stakes out a position of what the Nasdaq will do next. What is countercultural is refusing to chase performance and refusing to accept that rules have been thrown out that, when they resurface, will remind people (the hard way) that they were never obsolete.

SMALL CHANGES AND BIG OUTCOMES

I believe the biggest problem our culture has with dividend growth investing is that huge things happen *over time* and in *small increments*. Most successful businesses grow and succeed over a long period of time. Most portfolios accrue their results due to many things that take place over decades, not minutes.

Our social media–addicted, get-rich-quick, get-fit-quick, instant-gratification culture values things differently.

One of the things that is most compelling about dividend growth investing is how powerful the transformation is over time, yet how rare it is that such a transformation requires something dramatic to happen. I think of how the McDonalds $0.02 per share dividend in the 1970s must have been seen by investors then. Yet, the $7.44 annual dividend now, 3x that of the entire stock price back then, seems absolutely massive (and, indeed, it is one of the most profitable investments in history). The success dripped and dripped, and, yes, the transformation is big, powerful, and impactful now, but its path involved a wide array of small and incremental successes. Celebrating such a thing is countercultural.

MCDONALDS CORP (MCD)

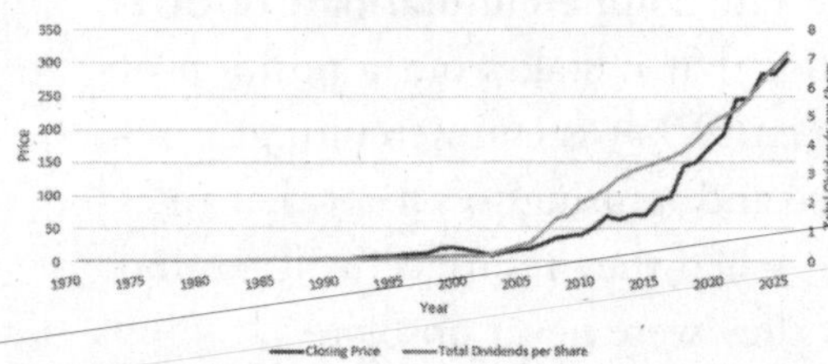

Note. Data is from Yahoo Finance for chart and tables.
https://finance.yahoo.com/quote/MCD/history/

Year	Total Dividends Per Share
1970	0.00
1971	0.00
1972	0.00
1973	0.00
1974	0.00
1975	0.00
1976	0.00
1977	0.00
1978	0.01
1979	0.01
1980	0.02
1981	0.02
1982	0.03
1983	0.04
1984	0.04
1985	0.05
1986	0.05
1987	0.06
1988	0.07
1989	0.08
1990	0.08
1991	0.09
1992	0.10
1993	0.11
1994	0.12
1995	0.13
1996	0.15
1997	0.16

Year	Total Dividends Per Share
1998	0.18
1999	0.20
2000	0.22
2001	0.23
2002	0.24
2003	0.40
2004	0.55
2005	0.67
2006	1.00
2007	1.50
2008	1.63
2009	2.05
2010	2.26
2011	2.53
2012	2.87
2013	3.12
2014	3.28
2015	3.44
2016	3.61
2017	3.83
2018	4.19
2019	4.73
2020	5.04
2021	5.25
2022	5.66
2023	6.23
2024	6.78
2025	7.17

The truth is that all compounding is subject to this dynamic—never feeling dramatic, but creating outcomes over time that are unrecognizable. So many things in our lives work this way, and it is a matter of character to embrace and celebrate them—the long victories versus the short and easy ones.

I would suggest that most of us have an example of this very thing in our own lives. The difference in my daughter from the beginning of kindergarten to the Christmas break of her kindergarten year was invisible. The change from kindergarten to first grade, and even from first grade to third grade, is small. But over time, these modest changes result in something we can't believe. The change from this little princess to this nineteen-year-old beauty did not come quickly. But the small changes resulted in a big and beautiful outcome.

CHAPTER FIVE

DEBUNKING THE FALLACY OF "GROWTH NOW, DIVIDENDS LATER"

"The best time to plant a tree was twenty years ago. The second-best time is now."
—Chinese proverb

AT MY FIRM, WE SOMETIMES hear from people who are sold on the benefits of dividend growth investing when it comes to their withdrawal phase of life, but want to try something different until then.

"Let me run up the score with Nvidia for now, and then I'll move to dividend growth when I am ready to begin withdrawing capital."

The idea is that they can accumulate a big capital base, an even bigger one than the compounding of a dividend growth portfolio would allow, and then "flip the switch" to a dividend growth withdrawal strategy for a "new phase" of their investing life.

It sounds good on paper. In real life, it is mistaken, mathematically errant, psychologically naive, and historically fallacious.

WHEN MATH BECAME FUN

I want to revisit the issue I wrote about in *The Case for Dividend Growth* regarding the epiphany that was "YOI"—the yield on original investment (some call it the "yield on cost," which is the same thing). It is common for an investor to look at the stock of a company that has been growing the dividend for a long time and see a current yield of 3 percent to 4 percent. Let's say that a stock price is $50 and the dividend is $2 per share (a 4 percent current yield). Now, let's say that this dividend grows 6 percent per year for thirty years. The dividend is now $11.49 ($2 compounded at 6 percent for thirty years). What are the odds that the annual yield on that stock in thirty years will be 23 percent (which is $11.49 divided by $50)? It is safe to say that the odds are very near $0. In fact, the yield might very well be 3 percent—lower than it was thirty years ago despite the fact that the dividend is up 575 percent in that time period. Why, you ask? Because the yield is the *math* of the *current dividend* divided by the *current price*. For the yield to be 23 percent, the stock would have had to stay level flat for thirty years. Now, some stock prices are where they were thirty years ago (I can tell you some tech stocks from the 1990s that *wish* they were where they were thirty years ago, and I can tell you some COVID-era darling stocks that will surely wish the same in another twenty-five years). But I already gave it away here—this hypothetical company grew the dividend by 6 percent for thirty years.

If we assume earnings grew by the same 6 percent to 7 percent over this period, the stock price would now be $380 (and if it split along the way, the math does not change; it just alters the price and number of shares but with the exact same economic value). So, if one looks at that company *today*, one would have an $11.49 dividend and a $380 stock price for a 3 percent current yield. So that 23 percent thing is all a façade, right?

It most certainly is not for the person who bought the company thirty years ago! I mean, yes, that person is up 6.6x on the $50 he paid for the stock (now worth $380 for an unrealized gain of $330), but he is literally receiving 23 percent per year on the money, as well. And over forty years, it is 40 percent in this hypothetical. And if you start using 7 percent or 8 percent or 9 percent annual increases in dividend, the numbers change so dramatically they sound unbelievable.

IT GETS EVEN BETTER

If I were being more honest, I would be less conservative in my illustrations, because the US stock market's great dividend growers are *filled* with companies that have done just that. In fact, what sold me on this math, enabling me to then become committed to the *concepts and facts* that created it, were example after example after example I encountered in the early careers of companies that were paying 100 percent or more *per year* to the owners of the original invested amount. The math blew me away. And yes, obviously, some massive capital gain had come with this, but it almost seemed like tip money compared to the sheer miracle of that compounded dividend.

The YOI became the most important number in investing finance for me. The idea that someone might get the amount he invested in the future *every single year,* and then die with all that money, a huge unrealized capital gain, blew me away. But unlike those high flyers and massive success stories in investing, "ten-baggers" and other such things, these stories of massive "yield on original investment" are incredibly common. This phenomenon is nothing more than mathematics that is far more "average" than meets the eye.

Consider this very abridged list of companies that currently have an annual dividend that is 100 percent to 400 percent of the actual stock price forty years ago:

Walmart
Home Depot
Lowe's
McDonald's
Coca-Cola
Altria Group
Procter & Gamble
Johnson & Johnson
Caterpillar
ExxonMobil
Colgate-Palmolive
Emerson Electric
PepsiCo
Conagra Brands
Archer Daniels Midland
Kimberly-Clark
Merck

This is not a list of stocks I am encouraging people to buy today, necessarily (though I do not mind sharing that, at press time, seven of these companies are in our company's dividend growth portfolio). It is provided informationally so that you will grasp the concept of *routine* companies that are not thought of as "high flyers" that have achieved a sort of investor nirvana—a 100 percent (or much more) annual cash flow on invested capital, without touching the principal, and ignoring the substantial gains in value that come therewith.

Of course, in a world of 3 percent to 5 percent bond yields and 1 percent to 2 percent S&P yields, one hardly needs a 100 percent to 400 percent YOI to ask where to sign up. The list of companies who are now offering a 20 percent or greater YOI just over the past fifteen years is stunning. It is also due to math.

CHICKEN OR THE EGG

The cause and effect here is very important. You could say, "Well, I guess those stock prices went up because the dividend went up," which is really another way of saying, "Stocks do not end up with 100 percent yields." In other words, if a company is growing its dividend 6 percent to 9 percent per year (The Bahnsen Group's target), and the dividend goes up as has been the case with this category of companies we are talking about, naturally the stock price went up with it. As the dividend increases, the price of the stock generally increases too. This sentence is true enough. But that is because of the *reason* why the dividends are increasing, which is to say, the growing profits are coming from good and defensible businesses. The profits are growing the value of the business; the dividend is giving investors a way to quantify the success of the business, all the while creating material, pocketable, verifiable, and consumable benefit to us, the risk-taker, the investor, the one with a future cash flow need.

The YOI is not a mathematical anomaly—it is a measurement of how dividends pull stock prices. From the prior hypothetical, that $380 current stock price with a 3 percent current yield doesn't tell us the operative bit of information; the 23 percent YOI does! Stock prices can go up when the company is not doing as well as we think; stock prices can go down when the company is doing better than we think; but the YOI tells us how our investment is doing—not the present snapshot of sentiment or resale value, but cash-on-cash. It transcends noise, chaos, information, sentiment, and psychology, and puts a quantitative measurement on the reality of our investment.[1]

HOPE IS NOT A STRATEGY

So, for those investors who want to benefit from the withdrawal stability of dividend growth and cash flow growth this strategy produces, but ignore the accumulation benefits, they play with the fire of denying the high YOI that is the aim of dividend growth accumulation. And they do so by replacing it with the strategy of hope that their accumulation period of unrealized gains will go as desired, and that the exit timing into a withdrawal strategy of dividend growth will play out as desired.

It is a delusion that comes from the most classic of behavioral mistakes imaginable.

1 It is important to note here that The Bahnsen Group's use of YOI as a practically important measurement does not imply that there are never reasons to sell stocks with a high YOI. Chapter Nine elaborates on the selling disciplines we use in an actively managed dividend growth portfolio.

First and foremost, it ignores the empirical reality that dividend growers have outperformed the broad index of the market over the timelines one thinks of as an "accumulation period."

DIVIDEND GROWERS: 50 YEARS OF OUTPERFORMANCE

Stocks of companies with growing free cash flow and rising dividends have historically provided solid returns with lower volatility.

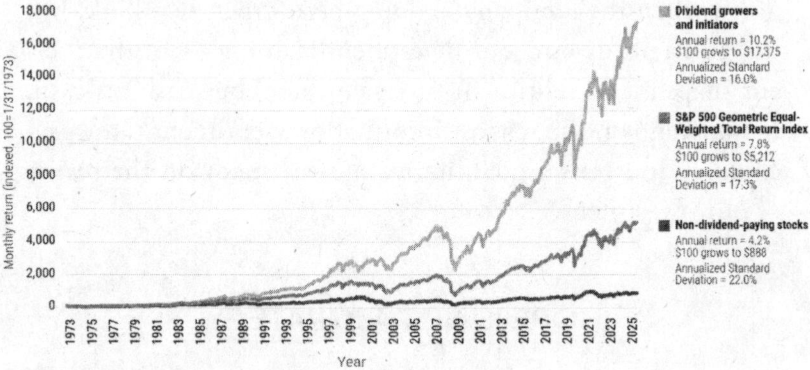

Source: Ned Davis Research for the period 01/31/73–12/31/2025. Data is updated annually.

RISK VS. RETURN, ANNUALIZED 1973-2024

Dividend Growth Stocks Have Outperformed With Less Risk

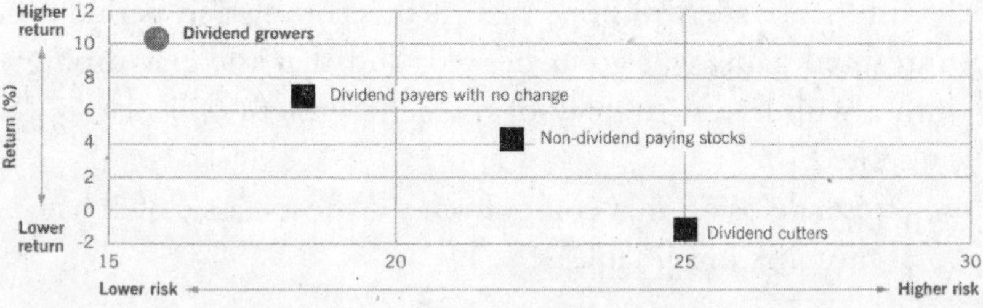

Data source: Nad Davis Research, Inc. and Refinitiv. 31 Jan 1973 – 31 Dec 2024. Further distribution prohibited without prior permission. Copyright 2025 © Ned Davis Research.

MISTAKES IN ACCUMULATION THINKING

Second, it presupposes that banking on multiple expansion is a smarter investment strategy than real-life cash flow expansion. That opportunity for "growth" to transcend cash flow is rooted in an argument in valuation and is especially seductive in the current moment of 23x stock markets. If the "growthier" areas of the market can see their price-to-earnings (P/E) ratios go from 20x to 40x, or from 30x to 60x, or if the whole stock market can go from 23x to 30x, the math seems to favor this aggressive approach. The rearview mirror of a S&P 500 that has gone from a mid-teen multiple after the financial crisis to its current 23x has enticed many people who say they get the appeal of dividend growth investing to play a game of chicken with the timing. Without conscious admission, the assertion is that one can get the timing of P/E valuation increase right more reliably than investors can receive growing dividends.

Third, it fails to appreciate the most opportunistic variable of compounding, and therefore compounding within compounding (dividend reinvestment on top of underlying company compounding): time.

Fourth, it naively assumes that if markets do not cooperate with their timeline and instead suffer a large drawdown before their withdrawal clock is to begin, that they will be psychologically willing to transition to a dividend withdrawal strategy, anyway. It misses that human nature loathes regret, and the regret of such timing hubris would almost surely cause investors to double down on such, compounding their risk, forfeiting opportunity, and delaying cash flow stability.

Fifth, it leans into the mistaken belief that dividend growth is merely an income strategy, instead of understanding that the income (receipt of dividends that are growing) is, itself, a by-product of growth. Robust earnings growth (and consequent stock price growth) is found in dividend growers. How do I know this? *Because no stock is yielding 100 percent, but many are yielding 100 percent at cost!!!*

Sixth (and I am well aware that many of these points overlap with one another), it replaces a strategy of company performance with a strategy of market psychology—of aligned investor sentiment. A dividend growth strategy focused on the dividend is 100 percent aligned with the operating performance of the company; believing that a "growth fund" or "index fund" or "tech heavy approach" will work *until the money is needed* requires the sentiment behind those valuations to hold. It is a timing call, and not one that has always ended well for people at the point that such timing issues can matter most.

HAVING YOUR CAKE AND EATING IT TOO

The base of capital that is creating income for an investor who needs current income matters. It is entirely understandable that one would want to focus more on withdrawal yield when one is withdrawing capital than when one is not. If I believed one could magically "optimize the capital base" without dividend growth, then "optimize the withdrawal protection and growth" with it, I would be all for it. But here is the logical inconsistency: If people believed they could do that in accumulation, why not believe they can do it in withdrawal? What is stopping them and their fortunate timing prowess from maintaining this "superior growth" throughout the withdrawal phase? They might say, "Well, I just don't want to risk it during the latter decades of my life," and that is a good answer—they shouldn't. But that very same vulnerability should not undermine the accumulation phase, either. I understand why some people would want to have their cake and eat it too; but I do not understand why anyone would believe such a thing would be advisable at any phase of an investor's life.

GETTING THE MENTALITY RIGHT

The reason to be in a dividend growth strategy at any phase of an investor's life is because you want your investment strategy to be focused on *profiting from profits.* Having a phase of life where that profiting is supercharged by the compounding of reinvestment is delightful and maximizing that window of time is a very good idea. When that reinvestment period (accumulation) has to end and the withdrawals have to begin, the mentality ought to be exactly the same: a vigilant focus on the fruit from the tree.

The mentality I advocate (and have committed my professional life to) is not to be turned on at one phase and seen as inferior in another. Generating reward as shareholders from receipt of growing dividends paid by outstanding companies aligned with their own investors is a philosophical orientation that is agnostic to accumulation versus withdrawal. Yes, the mechanics change operationally (reinvestment versus payment to cash), but the investment fundamentals are identical—and the opportunity cost for delay is severe.

CONCLUSION

Delaying dividend growth is to diminish its benefits and essentially undermine the strength and value of the strategy. Investors would be wise to remember that:

- When it comes to dividend growth, time is a force multiplier. If it is high future income you are after, the longer you compound dividend growth, the higher your YOI will be. That will be the future fruit that you eat.
- If it is growth you are after, buy companies that grow and give you more shares of ownership claims on their growth, each and every quarter. Your ownership grows. The company grows. The profits you participate in grow. Your share of those profits grow. Other than that, there is no growth going on here.
- To do something different, consciously, in the accumulation phase versus withdrawal phase, is to subconsciously invite a game of timing into your portfolio that is illogical and incoherent. Or, if I am being nicer, ill-advised.
- The tax efficiency of a "growth now, dividend portfolio later" strategy is, shall we say, sub-optimal.
- Dividend growth is a total return strategy that has empirically done better by that very standard than other available options. The mechanics change in withdrawal versus accumulation, but the philosophy of capital allocation does not.

- No one ever regretted letting dividend growth compound as an accumulation strategy. Many, many people regretted relying on market timing and valuation at a moment of moving to "withdrawal" mode. There is no timing risk to locking in YOI as a driver of portfolio value. There is significant risk to the alternative.

As I have said to my kids many times, there is never a wrong time to do the right thing. Markets do not run on your withdrawal schedule. Do not become an income investor at retirement; arrive at retirement owning a portfolio armed with the cash flow you need.

CHAPTER SIX

MORE THAN TOLERABLE—MAKING VOLATILITY YOUR FRIEND

"Volatility is the price of admission. The prize inside are superior long-term returns. You have to pay the price to get the returns."

—Morgan Housel

"Look at market fluctuations as your friend rather than your enemy; profit from folly rather than participate in it."

—Warren Buffett

THERE ARE THREE THINGS I believe those who make their living in the financial advisory profession are supposed to do about the portfolio volatility that is entirely assured if their clients are to be invested in anything but cash: (1) prepare them for it, (2) educate them about it, and (3) when it comes, remind them what they are *not* to do. This trio remains one of the cornerstones of a value proposition for a wealth advisor worthy of his or her fee, and it truly does encompass all three.

THE BASIC REALITY OF IT ALL

Most investors either want or need a return above what a savings account can provide. That risk premia is why investors build portfolios—to assemble the financial assets whose return will exceed the increase in cost of living that comes over time, along with the "premium" that a given client is seeking to fund his or her accumulation (note: future withdrawal) goals. As explained in this book's introduction, "accumulation" and "withdrawal" are the same thing—with the variables simply being timeline specifics and the mechanics of such withdrawal (periodic versus lump sum). We can add more nuance, such as how the recipient of such withdrawals might change (Mr. Smith might withdraw from Mr. Smith's portfolio for Mr. Smith's own retirement, or Mr. Smith's grandchildren's trustee might withdraw for his grandkids' education, or Mr. Smith's church might withdraw after his passing and a charitable bequest, but *someone* is withdrawing for *something*). The return the money earns between the point of investment and the use of the principal capital is what the purpose of investing is. Though, as you may recall from Chapter One, it is better to say that it is the result of investment; the purpose is the deployment of capital toward the production of goods and services that meet the needs of humanity. We are wise to remember this.

DEFINING RISK THOUGHTLESSLY

Back to the subject at hand. The "return above the cash rate" all investors pursue comes with various risks. Some high-risk options could entail a very high return—with the risk of "the money going away." Some face inflation risk and reinvestment risk (think of bond portfolios). But by far, the most common risk that public equity investors are faced with is something called "volatility," and it has created the most tragic distortion of vocabulary in the investment lexicon.

Volatility refers to the "up and down movement of price" that is entirely assured for public equity investment. Less liquid investments seem to have less exposure to volatility because the lack of mark-to-market pricing does not expose investors to the inherent volatility of their asset class. Real estate, private equity, and private credit would show fluctuations in price (volatility), too, if there was an active liquid market for those assets. In other words, those asset classes lack volatility to the extent we are talking about a basic tautology—that, by definition, something whose price can't change because there is no active buying and selling doesn't have its price change (no volatility). I can say this slower if it would help anyone.

Interest rates, inflation, investor sentiment, macroeconomic news, geopolitics, and, in some cases, the color of the sky can cause prices to move up or down on a daily (or nanosecond) basis. Since all asset classes have some degree of exposure to, well, interest rates, inflation, investor sentiment, macroeconomic news, geopolitics, and the color of the sky, all investors are exposed to such. That public equity investing is among the most liquid and efficient asset classes on the planet is, I was taught, a feature, not a bug. But when it comes to volatility, the heightened visibility of it is allegedly a bug. So much so, that an investing lexicon was created to prepare us for the "risk" of "volatility."

Embedded in almost every measurement of portfolio return is something called "standard deviation." Risk-adjusted returns are said to be a measurement of the return of a given portfolio divided by its standard deviation. "Standard deviation" is nothing more than the variance a portfolio is subject to around its own average return (volatility). The industry standard to measure risk-adjusted returns for institutional and retail investors, alike, is the Sharpe Ratio,[1] which essentially takes the portfolio return minus the risk-free rate, and divides such by the standard deviation of the portfolio. There certainly is relevance to the metric, and, all things being equal, it is entirely understandable why someone would like a 12 percent average return with no fluctuations to the downside at all *more* than a 12 percent average return with lots of fluctuation along the way. Even when the math ends up being the same, I do not discount that the emotional experience to get there may be very different for one portfolio versus another.

But that is not the same thing as "risk," which, by any rational person's definition, involves some element of failure. A permanent erosion of capital that leads to an inability to achieve a financial objective strikes me as a practical definition of risk. Volatility is not, in and of itself, the same, or even close to it. But the reason I started this chapter with a reminder of the solemn charge given to all in the advisory profession is that volatility can lead to "risk of failure" if it becomes so

---

1 Other measurements include the Treynor ratio, which does the same thing as the Sharpe ratio but uses the portfolio beta instead of standard deviation, and the Sortino ratio, which divides the excess return of the portfolio by just the do*wnside* volatility of the portfolio. All such measurements have one main thing in common: a presumption that "risk" and "volatility" are the same thing.

unsettling that it causes an investor to abandon their own investment plan. My experience is that people are much less inclined to be disturbed by things they knew were coming (as opposed to things that amount to the element of surprise), hence, the duty of preparation. Merely telling a person that "there will be volatility" may not be enough, though, so the education is important too. Using historical reality and empirical facts to paint the picture should help—and certainly reinforce—the goal of preparation.

S&P 500 INTRA-YEAR DECLINES VS. CALENDAR YEAR RETURNS

DESPITE AVERAGE INTRA-YEAR DROPS OF 14.2%, ANNUAL-RETURNS WERE POSITIVE IN 35 OF THE 46 YEARS

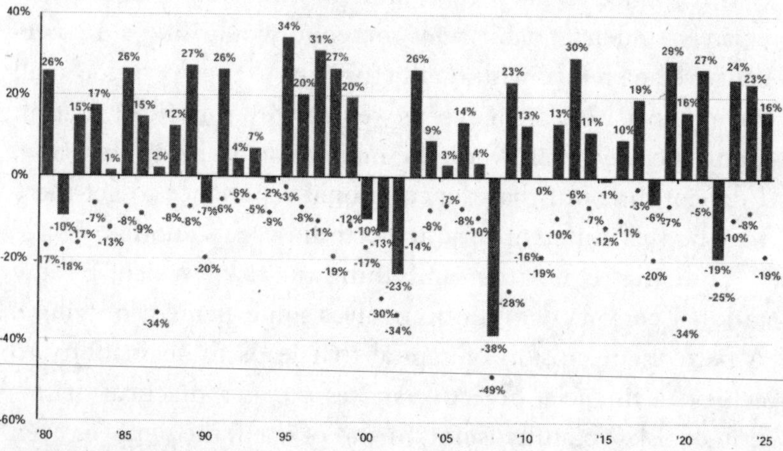

Source: FactSet, Standard & Poor's, J.P. Morgan Asset Management.
Returns are based on price index only and do not include dividends. Intra-year drops refers to the largest peak-to-trough decline during the year. Returns shown are calendar year returns from 1980 to 2025, over which the average annual return was 10.7%. Past performance is no guarantee of future results.
Guide to the Markets – U.S. Data are as of December 31, 2025.

J.P.Morgan ASSET MANAGEMENT

A QUICK CAVEAT

I have thus far referred to volatility, whether reasonably benign fluctuations like the routine ones we see every month, quarter, and year in investing, or more severe ones like those outlier events that happen every four or five years on average (bear markets, recessions, and world events), as something that only becomes a threat to the goals of the investor to the extent it causes an investor to behave badly, hence making the real risk the investor, and not the portfolio volatility. But, it should be said, this is only true for unlevered investors. I was struck by this statement from the alpha-generating machine of a hedge fund investor Bill Ackman: "Volatility is the friend of the *unleveraged* long-term investor. We much prefer the bumpy road to higher rates of return than a smoother ride to more modest profits." (Emphasis added.)

He is acknowledging the financial market tautology that enhanced expected rates of return come from enhanced volatility. This is a fundamental tenet of the capital asset pricing model and does, indeed, capture the math of investing: Investors will take a lower rate of return when the ride there is less volatile, and will demand a higher rate of return when the ride there is more volatile. Therefore, higher rates of return can be found where the tolerance of volatility is higher (at least, theoretically).

But look at the word I emphasized in the Ackman quote: unleveraged. The math of using borrowed money to acquire assets with a positive rate of return means that an investor's own behavior is not the sole determinant of their staying power, but it invites the cooperation of their lender. Portfolio lenders who provide the debt to "leverage" investor returns (borrowed money to provide more juice to the upside) have formulaic rules for their selling decisions. Put differently, high volatility can unwind a good portfolio where there is leverage, no matter what the investor's behavior or appetite for volatility may be. Margin clerks are not persuadable by the tenets of behavioral modification.

The perspective on volatility I have embraced in this chapter, but also throughout my career and practice, presupposes that an investor actually has control of his own response to portfolio volatility. Leverage requires a surrender of such control to the math of margin-borrowing rules—and changes everything.

NAVIGATING HUMAN NATURE

Yet, as any professional advisor can attest, both *preparation* and *education* have limits when it comes to human nature. *Navigation* through such things is intensely personal, psychological, and emotional. Such navigation will not be too intense during routine volatility, especially if the right preparation and education was done, but during more severe volatility, many rules are thrown out when fear enters the picture. In these situations, "volatility" may very well seem to be synonymous with "risk" just because the investor's own propensity to behave in a way that puts his own objectives at risk is so elevated. In that practical sense, I understand why volatility matters, but it is less about volatility doing damage to the goals of the investor and more about the investor doing damage to himself or herself, because of the emotional response to volatility. This dynamic is not mentioned as a critique of human nature; it is a description of an immutable truth. And, I believe it leads to two major takeaways that are true for every investor:

1. As much as possible, the volatility potential of a given investor's portfolio ought to be constrained by that

investor's true emotional tolerance for a bandwidth of downside fluctuation. This is not measurable by asking an investor, "What is your tolerance for a bandwidth of downside fluctuation?" mostly because that is jargon-filled nonsense, but also because an investor's emotional comforts, themselves, change with circumstances. That one can *say* one is comfortable with a 20 percent decline in prices in the middle of a bull market where one does not really believe such is possible is unhelpful in assessing one's real comfort level once a major market disruption occurs (not if, but when).

2. Because of the challenges described above in using an investor's own answers to create volatility bandwidth comfort levels, it remains incumbent on a fiduciary advisor to be that last ballast for the investor—to do all within the advisor's legal, moral, and personal ability to keep the investor from undermining his own success by capitulating to the panic or euphoria that will take over any investor's emotions (and then behavior) without appropriate counsel and intervention. To this end, the advisory profession either works, or it perishes.

ADDING TO THE TOOLBOX

Yet, I will propose a third dynamic that is too often ignored when discussing volatility, and that is the concept of making volatility a genuine friend to your portfolio results, an aid to the premium of total return you seek, an accomplice to the achievement of your financial goals. You will note in the first quote at the beginning of this chapter that the brilliant Morgan Housel presents volatility as something to be tolerated in exchange for the premium returns that inherently volatile asset classes (like public equities) contain. He is not wrong—volatility is an entrance ticket for the desired aim. From Buffett to Housel to a who's who of investing geniuses, volatility is defended as it should be (and as I have already done in this chapter): as the inevitable accomplice to a good portfolio in pursuit of a premium return. It may be a psychological hassle, an emotional burden, and a testing of the natural humanity we all bring to investing, but it is not the same thing as risk. As long as investors behave rationally (especially with the preparation, education, and navigation of a competent and empathetic financial professional), volatility need not do harm.

I am 100 percent on board with all of this.

But might I suggest that dividend growth investing goes one step further. It creates an embedded, systematic, automatic, nonemotional, and mathematical way for investors to benefit from the reality of volatility. It does not suspend the need for preparation, education, and navigation, but it does add a bit of capitalization to the mix. Investors can capitalize on portfolio volatility with dividend growth in a way other volatile portfolio strategies in public equities cannot.

CRUCIAL CLARITY

That I am not wrong in my claim that dividend growth equities benefit from portfolio volatility in no way minimizes the need for the aforementioned preparation, education, and navigation. Dividend growth equities suffer bear markets too. Dividend growth equities are subject to the laws of the universe too. Recessions, bear markets, global pandemics, terrorist attacks, financial crises, trade wars, and even the far dumber reasons for market declines affect dividend growth companies too. Do I believe that the price impact is much less than that of the price impact on non-dividend growing companies? I do, and that is supposed to be self-attesting by the lower beta of a dividend growth portfolio. Beta measures market sensitivity, and so if something has a lower sensitivity to the market, you expect it to be less sensitive to the market when the market gets in a bad mood. (You have no idea how much of what I do for a living is merely to defend the actual meaning of words in the English language.)

DIVIDEND GROWTH IS ALSO PROTECTIVE ON THE DOWNSIDE

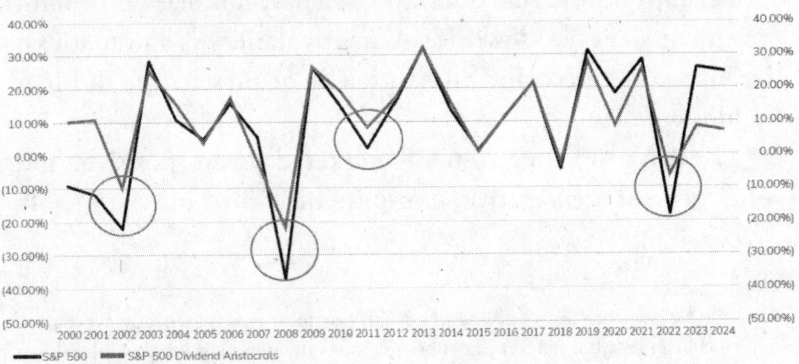

DIVIDEND GROWERS

- +10.10% per year
  S&P 500: +7.61% per year
- +1,007.16% cumulative
  S&P 500: +525.24% cumulative
- 14.26% Volatility
  S&P 500: 15.28% Volatility
- Outperformed the S&P 500 16 of 25 years and 53% of months since 2000

*Data Source: FactSet

But despite a perhaps lesser violence of volatility for dividend growth equities in most instances of market disruption,[2] there still exists real inherent volatility because we are still talking public equities. Dividend growth stocks are stocks (there we go again with these tautologies), and the very nature of things subjects them to some inherent volatility, and a serious need for proper investor behavior around such.

WITH THAT SAID

The unpredictable nature of market volatility leads to a situation where long-term investors with a diversified portfolio of dividend-growing stocks cannot help but receive dividends throughout their investing lives (reinvested in shares of the same company paying the dividend) at all sorts of different prices (up, down, and sideways). That accumulation of reinvestment shares in downside market volatility is automatic; it is outside the need for human talent or prescience, and it is wildly opportunistic.

Roughly 53.7 percent of market days are positive, and 46.3 percent are negative, not quite fifty–fifty, but reasonably

2 In my own career as a dividend growth portfolio manager, nearly every period I can recall of market drawdown saw our dividend growth portfolio down much less than the market's drawdown itself. In some instances (the 2022 bear market comes to mind), our dividend growth portfolio was up even as the market declined over 20 percent. That said, one exception will not ever be forgotten, which was the COVID-19 sell-off in the middle of 2020. In that case, an overweight to energy hurt returns while the underweight to non-dividend paying technology stocks as everyone stayed home streaming and buying things online also hurt returns. But even that was a rare underperformance in a time of downside volatility, as energy became the best-performing sector in the year that followed.

close.[3] As the timeline pulls out more, we see about 60 percent of months being positive, and about 69 percent of quarters being positive. Most companies pay their dividends quarterly. What we have here is a mathematical statement that 31 percent of the time, dividends will be paid at a lower price than the prior quarter. But not every company follows the same dividend payment timeline, which means some might pay the first, fourth, seventh, and tenth months of the year, but others pay the second, fifth, eighth, and eleventh, while yet others pay the third, sixth, ninth, and twelfth. In other words, an organically diversified portfolio is going to have dividends paying every month, and about 40 percent of market months are down versus the month before. Before we get to any extended market drawdowns, dividend growth accumulators are "taking advantage of volatility" about 40 percent of the time, just by being invested.

Now imagine a two-year bear market (1973–1974), or a 2000 market that does not recapture its high until 2007. Or a 2008 market sell-off that does not recapture its pre-crisis high until 2013. And imagine adding new shares to your own stocks in your own portfolio at lower prices quarter after quarter after quarter. The volatility is survivable by all. Indeed, it is the "price of admission"—but with dividend growth, it is not merely "survivable" but actually creating a far, far better long-term result than if we hadn't had the volatility at all!

I gave up trying to convince clients to root for bear markets long ago, but I have at least made progress convincing them that there is a real "bright side" to downside market

---

3 Crestmont Research, "Percentage Positive and Negative Days Across Various Periods: S&P 500 Index," 2025, https://www.crestmontresearch.com/docs/Stock-Yo-Yo.pdf.

volatility. And while the emotions and psychology of opening our statements or looking at closing values online does not lend itself to us enjoying it all, the math of it is crystal clear: dividend growth accumulation investors benefit from sustained market declines.

Stock price declines with a dividend that does not decline will allow you to increase the yield of your portfolio (because of math). All of the accumulation at lower prices is the exact same thing as "accumulation at higher yield" (they are mathematically inversed to one another). The additional shares increase the future yield *both* by nature of the higher yield at which shares were purchased *and* the additional shares now paying a dividend to shareholders. This income-driven averaging is self-reinforced compounding in any market environment, but in a volatile market, it is optimal.

CONCLUSION

Behaviorally, any decline in prices could lead to bad decisions, without the right preparation, education, and navigation. But when an investor understands that the by-product of downside volatility in his portfolio is capitalization, he is far less threatened (emotionally) by the difficult times, and far better off (mathematically) in the dividend-paying power of his portfolio. I also believe that stable dividend growers will generally suffer less than names whose stock price appreciation is more dependent on multiple expansion (one of the defining characteristics of a down market is declining market multiples, and the P/E ratios that tend to decline the most are the ones that were most elevated or stretched). Yet, I would suggest that this is merely an anecdotal cushion of comfort in the grand scheme of things, and that the real benefit for dividend growth investors is not merely the "less marginal discomfort," but the "greater marginal opportunity."

And with enough time and enough volatility, this opportunity is far more than "marginal." It is life changing.

Volatility does not change the long-term reality of a durable business. But it does change the terms on which we buy such businesses. And it changes those terms in our favor when we are dividend growth investors.

CHAPTER SEVEN

THE TAX ARGUMENT TURNED UPSIDE DOWN

"Friends and neighbors complain that taxes are indeed very heavy, and if those laid on by the government were the only ones we had to pay, we might more easily discharge them; but we have many others, and much more grievous to some of us. We are taxed twice as much by our idleness, three times as much by our pride, and four times as much by our folly."

—Benjamin Franklin

IT IS ENTIRELY RATIONAL THAT investors want to optimize their returns on an *after-tax* basis. We speak of *real* returns (versus nominal ones) as the return that is net of *inflation*. In other words, if an investor earns 10 percent in a year but the cost of living (in some broad and reasonable measurement) has gone up 2 percent, we speak of the *nominal* return as being 10 percent but the *real* return being 8 percent, because that is real to the investor. Likewise, if an investor earns 10 percent, loses 2 percent to inflation, and another 2 percent, 3 percent, or 4 percent to taxes, the real, after-tax return is perhaps closer to 6 percent, 5 percent, or 4 percent. Regardless of what the particular numbers are based on actual changes in the price level and actual impact of taxes, the point is: what investors care about is what they get to keep after all is said and done.

This should be rather obvious.

AN EXCEPTION FOR THE BERNIE BROS

I suppose I should allow for the caveat that some people may believe in big government spending and taxation so much that they consider their pre-tax return to be all that matters to them, and, in fact, consider the higher tax burden they incur from investment return to be a feature, not a bug. Based on the way many speak and argue, this would be consistent with their rhetoric, but I have not found it to be a *modus operandi* of very many investors. In fact, it has been my experience that some of the biggest advocates of higher tax rates for investors and business owners are among the most aggressive in pursuing what they delicately refer to as "tax efficiency."[1] I

1 While Warren Buffett is perhaps the greatest investor who ever lived, this will always be something that confuses me to no end about his legacy. He has spent decades bemoaning lower tax rates on investment and supporting high estate tax burdens, yet has consistently managed his own portfolio with an extraordinary focus on "tax efficiency" and touted that tax efficiency publicly. Likewise, he has worked tirelessly to minimize his own estate tax burden with various philanthropic and tax strategies, all of which are legal and entirely appropriate. I have no problem at all with Buffett's actions; just confusion when it comes to the mismatch between his words and his actions.

begrudge no one for seeking to minimize his own tax burden as long as it is done legally, though I confess to being confused when one who claims to want a higher tax burden for his class of earner would seek such mitigation when he can absolve his own guilt by merely bypassing opportunities that limit taxable consequence.

But I digress.

WHAT ENDS UP IN YOUR POCKET

So, pre-tax returns (before tax considerations) and nominal returns (before inflation considerations) are a starting point, but not an ending point, for real-life investors who are not pharisees or masochists. After-tax real returns are the returns that matter to investors. The impact of taxes on dividend growth investors has been the subject of much discussion over the years. Like many subjects in investing, that discussion is often not only misconstrued, but also entirely reversed from cogent consideration.

In this chapter, I do not merely argue that the way dividends are taxed is not the problem some suggest it is, but that it is a tremendous benefit compared to the alternative. Put differently, I am not arguing that the tax reality of dividend stocks is an acceptable burden; I am arguing that it is an argument for dividend growth investing.

IN A PERFECT WORLD

I have no problem saying that, ideally, I would like investors to keep 100 cents of every dollar they receive, and likewise in capital gains. After-tax dollars that get invested are, well, already taxed dollars (hence the term "after tax"). Someone earned the funds, paid income taxes on the wages, and then, with those dollars, put them into a savings account, a bond, a stock, a fund, or some other form of savings and investment. The consequence of that savings or investment activity generates a return (whether it be in interest income, a coupon payment from a bond, a realized gain from a profitable asset sale, or a dividend from a stock). This investment activity is then taxed at the tax rate that goes with that particular investment category (interest income from savings, money markets, and bonds are taxed as ordinary income; qualified dividends and long-term capital gains are taxed at more favorable investment tax rates).[2] As a matter of economic philosophy, I believe lower tax rates on investment would spur greater investment, and greater investment would create more jobs and produce more economic growth, enhancing the tax base and facilitating a better result for all. Indeed, reduced tax rates on investment have always led to greater total receipts in tax revenue for government (under Presidents Coolidge, Kennedy, Reagan, Clinton, and Bush) following said reduction in tax rates. I am not suggesting that wealthy investors should pay lower taxes on their wages than all other wage earners. In fact,

2 Dividends and long-term capital gains are currently taxed at a 15 percent rate up to $545,500 of income and then 20 percent above that level (for singles), and 15 percent up to $613,700 of income and then 20 percent above that level (for married couples). Those with incomes below $49,450 (single) or $98,900 (married) pay no tax on dividends or capital gains. There is also something called a Net Investment Income Tax (NIIT) of 3.8 percent applied to those with a modified adjusted gross income above $200,000 (single) or $250,000 (married). This NIIT is commonly known as the Obamacare surtax, passed as part of the Affordable Care Act in 2010. It is, therefore, common to think of the federal dividend and capital gains tax rate as 23.8 percent, where the investor is in a high tax bracket and has high levels of investment income.

the income tax rates are highly progressive, and the top end of wage earners pay an extremely disproportionate amount of total taxes relative to total wages earned.[3] What I am suggesting, though, is that once income has been earned (and taxed), the secondary tax that is applied to the earnings on those after-tax dollars should be as low as possible—if our goal as a society is to incentivize more investment and savings, which is the bedrock of capital formation, which is the key ingredient in driving productivity, growth, and ultimately, a better standard of living for all.

So, yes, if Mr. Smith could sell his Apple stock at a $10,000 gain and keep all $10,000 of it, and if Mrs. Smith could receive $10,000 of dividends on her JP Morgan stock and keep all $10,000 of it, that would be optimal in Daveland. But alas, it is not the current tax code, and my reading of the tea leaves does not cause me to believe it is going to be anytime soon.

Our job as investors is to invest for what is, not for what ought to be. This applies to how we think about monetary policy, company decision-making, the macroeconomic landscape, and, yes, tax policy.

EQUAL FOOTING WHEN PROPERLY UNDERSTOOD

You will note from the prior section that dividends and capital gains are taxed at the same rate in the current tax code. Whether Mr. Smith falls into a 0 percent investment tax

3 Erica York, "Summary of the Latest Federal Income Tax Data, 2025 Update," Tax Foundation, November 18, 2024, https://taxfoundation.org/data/all/federal/latest-federal-income-tax-data-2025/.

bracket, a 15 percent investment tax bracket, or a 20 percent investment tax bracket, he would be paying the same tax on qualified dividends and long-term capital gains. There is a difference between investment tax rates and earned-income tax rates, but that is not what people refer to when talking about the burden of dividend taxation (especially since investment tax rates are *lower* than earned income tax rates). There also is a difference between the tax treatment of, say, rental income, interest income, and bond income, as well as investment income, but again, those differences are *favorable* to those receiving dividends, not unfavorable. Those various categories of interest income are taxed as part of ordinary income rates which are subject to higher tax rates.

So, what are people referring to in trying to pit dividend taxation as sub-optimal if dividend income is taxed at a lower rate than earned income and all of the investment strategies that are taxed as ordinary income? If dividends and (long-term) capital gains are taxed exactly the same, what is the problem?

Dividends are received year-by year and therefore taxed year-by-year, whereas capital gains are taxed only in the year that they are incurred.

In other words, capital gains (and therefore the tax on capital gains) can be zero so long as they are kept "unrealized" (or so the thinking goes). Dividends will be taxed in the year they are received, but if an investor avoids those pesky dividends in favor of stocks that go up in value but never get sold they can increase their after-tax return.

What could go wrong?

A QUALIFIER

The prior paragraph does reference the equal footing between tax treatment on *qualified* dividends and capital gains, so a quick *qualifier* is in order on what constitutes a qualified dividend. The "investment tax" treatment (0 percent, 15 percent, or 20 percent, depending on income bracket) applies to long-term capital gains and *qualified* dividends. To meet the definition of a *qualified* dividend, the dividend must be paid by a US corporation, or, if a foreign corporation, it must meet certain IRS criteria. The investor must also hold the stock more than sixty days during the 121-day period beginning sixty days before the ex-dividend date. In other words, from sixty days before the ex-dividend date to sixty days after that date, the investor must hold the stocks for sixty of those days. Simple enough.

So, besides a holding period and tax domicile of the payer, what could make a dividend "non-qualified" (that is, taxed at ordinary income rates versus more favorable investment rates)? Well, very often, the distributions of foreign companies are treated as nonqualified. The distributions from business development companies (BDCs) are nonqualified. The dividends from real estate investment trusts (REITs) and master limited partnerships (MLPs) are nonqualified. However, it is important to remember with REITs that the income being passed through to shareholders has not been taxed at the corporate level, so there is a different tax advantage involved. MLPs also involve depreciation and other shelters that render that tax treatment more favorable, as well (with much of the distribution often treated as return of capital for tax purposes). The final category generally considered nonqualified are dividends paid to employee stock.

LIMITING THE CONVERSATION

We should first clear the field a bit. Nothing we are talking about in this chapter applies to where well above 50 percent of US investor assets are held: tax-advantaged retirement accounts.[4] Whether it be a 401(k) account made available by one's employer, a ROTH IRA, a traditional IRA, or a rollover IRA (where an investor moves past 401(k) accounts when he or she leaves a job), all such accounts do not incur tax on investment activity. Rather, if the account was funded with pre-tax dollars, the tax is based on the withdrawal amount (regardless of how the money grew along the way), and if the account was funded with after-tax dollars (a ROTH IRAs or a 401(k), for example), there is no tax on the investment activity or the withdrawal. Therefore, the tax treatment on dividends is wholly irrelevant to the entire discussion for well more than half of US investor dollars.

But even in regular taxable accounts, there is another group for whom this entire discussion is irrelevant—and that is the sizable percentage of investors who take regular withdrawals and periodic distributions from their account. Indeed, unless that investor is withdrawing from a *realized loss* (which would represent a negative after-tax real return), he

4 Elizabeth A. Myers, "Ownership of Retirement Accounts in 2022: Amounts in Defined Contribution Plans and Individual Retirement Accounts," Congressional Research Service Report No. R48143, July 29, 2024, https://www.congress.gov/crs-product/R48143, and Investment Company Institute, September 18, 2025.

is presumably withdrawing *either* from a *realized capital gain* or else a *dividend*, both of which are taxed at exactly the same tax rate. If income-oriented investors had the option of paying a lower tax rate on capital gains against a higher tax rate on dividends, there may be some need for deeper calculation here. But since the tax rates are identical for both, periodic withdrawers of capital not only have the superior investment mechanics with dividends that I outlined in Chapter Two, as well as superior protection against sequence-of-returns risk outlined in Chapter Three, but would also have completely equal tax treatment.[5]

So, the discussion at hand legislatively eliminates the investments in tax-advantaged retirement accounts and logistically eliminates the investments in after-tax accounts from which one needs to regularly withdraw capital. That leaves just one category of investment/investor for whom this discussion has relevance: the long-term accumulator who is accumulating in an after-tax account.

PRIMA FACIE ACCEPTABILITY OF THE ARGUMENT

The math makes sense. One investor receives $10,000 of dividends and has unrealized appreciation of $10,000. The other investor has $0 of dividends and has unrealized appreciation

5 I am trying to avoid making this overly complicated, but it is only "equal" tax treatment on capital gains and dividends if you assume (which I am doing for the sake of argument in this chapter) that all the capital gains realized would be long-term—that is, on investments held for longer than one year. In reality, it is entirely possible that a withdrawer of capital might need to realize gains on positions held for less than one year at times, creating a leakage where the tax burden becomes worse with realized capital gains than with dividends.

of $20,000. The tax for Investor A is $2,000, meaning she has an after-tax return of $18,000, while the tax for Investor B is $0, meaning he has an after-tax return of $20,000. All that an investor has to do to get a $2,000 higher after-tax return ($2,000 of $20,000, so 10 percent better) is avoid companies that dare to return profits to them.

Good in theory. Highly problematic in practice.

A FUTURE LIABILITY WHEN YOU LEAST WANT ONE

Of course, very few investors are investing merely for the dollars they intend to die with; there is some capital return objective attached to the dollars they are accumulating. If they give investments that have an unrealized gain away in their lifetime, the person they give them to will pay the capital gain tax when he or she sells (this includes placing the investments in irrevocable trusts that will not receive a step-up at death). If investors want to accumulate capital for years or even decades, and then withdraw for various future spending needs (the most common accumulation objective), all they will have done is push the tax liability into the future—not reduce it—and, in fact, will have almost guaranteed a sub-optimal outcome for themselves.

Selling stock with a massive capital gain to fund retirement is, shall we say, not easy for people to do, both psychologically and economically. The best performers over time have the highest gains, and therefore the highest tax consequence to redeem, and therefore, the most reasons for an investor to, in the future, find reasons to avoid selling. Over and over and over again, this results in a portfolio heavily distorted by the psychologically driven decisions of avoiding a given tax impact. Now, avoiding a tax impact is, in and of itself, perfectly rational. But is there any reason whatsoever to believe that in ten years or twenty years, what is best for one's portfolio will be to heavily overweight the stocks that did best many years earlier? It may *seem* to make sense ("I am limiting tax consequence") but *does it* make sense? Has history ever concluded that such a decision was ill-advised? I think the question is better phrased as: has history ever *not* punished an investor for doing this?

Besides the fact that the entire idea presupposes that a company never returning capital to its shareholders, or only doing so via stock buybacks, is a good thing for investors—a presupposition that I recommend fighting with every ounce of energy you can muster—even the basic, fictional apples-to-apples scenario of equal returns with one being all in unrealized gains, and one in dividends, fully misses the point of what is taking place for accumulators. The "unrealized gain, no dividend investor" is accumulating a large future liability—the tax burden such investors will incur in the future, unless they choose to avoid such by making very bad investment decisions. The dividend investor has not only been in a much more sensible portfolio along the way, achieving all the benefits described in prior chapters about company capital discipline and investor compounding, but the dividend investor has avoided the creation of a handcuff on his future portfolio in the form of disincentives and decision distortions around a large accumulated unrealized gain.

The dividend investor, after accumulating a substantial tree generating substantial fruit, can merely start taking the fruit, and not have the sizable tax burden of having to cut part of the tree down to fund future spending needs. And he can do this without playing the mental games *all* investors end up playing when they face such a large capital gain burden—"You know, I really shouldn't sell this because..."

I do not have to describe this risk hypothetically because I have encountered it in real life for more than twenty-five years. From one's own residence to all sorts of investment real estate decisions to a stock portfolio, tax consequences alter decisions all the time. What a dividend investor does is achieve the returns he or she wants along the way, unfortunately having to pay taxes due to the laws of the land, yes, but without leaving himself or herself with a daunting and difficult decision tree that looms over future financial peace and wisdom. This, my friends, is a feature, not a bug.

If an investor is going to have to monetize later one way or the other, dividends become a far better way to do so for all the investment reasons we have discussed, and without building a massive tax liability when one most needs investment flexibility. The alternative limits flexibility and creates poor decision-making, or, best case, renders decisions harder than they ought to be. The dividend growth tax treatment facilitates the flexibility investors ought to have.

It can be put rather simply this way: As long as dividends and capital gains have identical statutory tax rates (they do), we are not talking about what is less or more in tax burden—we are talking about whether or not you will actually want the money. If you will, do you like the idea of deteriorating from the tree in the future, or having flexibility and optionality at the stage of your investing life where you most need it? Does "paying as you go" sound better than being handcuffed to potentially bad decisions, concentration risk, and selective rationalizations in your portfolio?

Dividend growth investing is a tool for avoiding the pigeonholing of your portfolio to tax consequences.

THE REAL HEART OF THE MATTER

I do not believe in letting the tax tail wag the investment dog, but I certainly understand focusing on optimizing one's real, after-tax returns. The tax consequences of dividend growth investing create benefits relative to alternatives unless one creates scenarios that are wholly unrealistic, Pollyannaish, and outside the risk constraints most investors want. But at the heart of this is the question of what dividend growth investing is throughout the accumulation phase—the auto-compounding machine around great companies with aligned management that gives you measurable rewards for the risk you take year, by year, by year.

Dividends reduce reliance on market timing, investor sentiment (multiple expansion), and future buyer appetite. Tax implications matter, but so do risk implications, as well as portfolio quality implications. If a company's reinvestment does not come at the same incremental returns as what created the profits to begin with, you are worse off not receiving the dividends, regardless of the tax consequences.

And yes, until Congress changes the tax code, those rewards have some tax associated with them, as any successful investment strategy does. The greatest way to avoid tax on investments is to have an unsuccessful investment plan.

Sadly, that is what many are actually doing, even if they don't realize it now. But whether it be a future tax liability or the awareness of a poor investment plan, they will "realize" it later.

It has been said that the only things guaranteed in life are death and taxes. When an entire investment return is contingent upon deferred gains—the hope of a future realization—an investor is voluntarily avoiding the guarantee of a positive benefit available along the way. Taxes are guaranteed, anyway. Investors would be wise to receive the "bird in the hand" of dividends versus the alternative. Because the only thing that avoids taxes for the alternative is no bird in the hand. The choice is easy.

CHAPTER EIGHT

THE ONLY QUESTION IS HOW TO RETURN CAPITAL TO OWNERS

"I don't like stock buybacks. I think if a company has the money to buy their stock back, then they should take that and increase the dividends. Send it back to the stockholder. Let them invest their money again from the dividends."

—T. Boone Pickens

"The very attention we place on rising dividends puts us squarely in the position of 'owners' of a company, of true investors who understand that a satisfying and reasonable return from a stock investment isn't a gift of the market or luck... but it is the logical and inevitable result of investing in a company that is actually doing well enough, in the real world, to both pay dividends and to increase them on a regular basis."

—Lowell Miller

WHAT IS THE VALUE OF A BUSINESS?

The "first principles" approach to investing that I began this book with and that encompasses all we do in managing money at my firm requires us to understand a very basic thing before we can understand anything about investing: What makes a company more valuable in the future than the present? Would you ever buy stock in a company you did not believe would be more valuable in the future than at the time you invested? Because that question answers itself, it seems to be pretty reasonable to know the answer to the first question—what is the reason a company would be more valuable in the future than the present? The answer is, always and forever, the belief that its profits will grow in the future. Profits drive the value of a company, and any exception one ever comes up with to this ironclad law of corporate finance is no exception at all. ("I believe it will be more valuable regardless of its profits because another company will want to buy it at a higher price.")

Why would another company buy it for a higher price other than the belief that its brand, assets, or strategic positioning would make *its own profits* go higher? ("I believe the assets the company accumulates will be worth more in the future.")

If by "assets" you mean the factories, equipment, plants, buildings, and other fixed assets, you better also have some sort of operating business or strategy attached to those assets (you know, the thing that creates "profits"), because otherwise, all you'll have is a balance sheet of *depreciating* assets generating nothing productive or profitable—a declining value over time (if divorced from an operating model).

We can play all the word games and do all the speculative maneuvering we want, but companies are worth more in the future when they earn more money, or when we believe they are about to earn more money. Period. This is the "first principle" of value creation: When you meet a human need, when you create value for others, profits are what follow. If you have goods or services that others want and an efficient way to deliver those goods or services, you have created value for others. If the most they will pay you for these goods or services is less than your cost of production, you will go out of business and you will have a business worth nothing. But chances are that if you have already created value for others in the goods or services you offer, they will pay you more than your cost of production, and that is what we call profits. And when those profits are sustainable, or believed to be sustainable, we have a real business. If the business has no path to profitability—to delivering value for a price above its cost—the business will fail.

DISCOUNTING THE FUTURE INTO THE PRESENT

If the business has achieved profitability, we get to value the business on some sort of projection around those future profits. Sometimes we have absolutely no way to imagine how large the profits will grow in the future—how many new products and services a company will develop, how many new markets a company might create for selling its goods and services, how many uses a company might find for its brand, technology, and platform. Discounting future cash flows to a present value can be tough when a company might shoot the lights out in terms of what its future profits could be, but that sounds like a pretty good problem to have. But if Benjamin Graham and Warren Buffett taught us anything, it is that if we know a company will generate $100 per year for the next ten years in profits, then we have $1,000 of value on our hands, provided it is discounted to a reasonable hurdle rate or discount rate.[1] If that $100 of profits in year one is going to grow each year based on cost reductions, expansions of locations, improved margins, or new products, then the expected profits will be higher, and the discounting of those future profits into a net present value leads to an even higher valuation.

This is, essentially, what the stock market is doing, all day, every day—with the added (highly distortive) component of investor sentiment and liquidity added in—discounting expectations for the future into the present. Once I learned to understand public markets as *discounting mechanisms*, it dramatically improved my abilities as an investor. One could say, "Company A is growing a lot and doing really well," and believe one has said something about the company's investment merits, but one would be wrong. If that growth and performance has already been discounted, or worse, *excessively* discounted, the price paid in the present might be too high for what the future profits are going to be. Of course, if a company's performance is going to *outperform* the discounting expectations of markets in the future, that current price might be very attractive for the future value.

So, always and forever, the thing that matters for value in the future is profits, and the other ingredient to performance will be the price paid for those profits.

---

1 A discount rate or hurdle rate could be the "risk-free" rate—that is, the return that an investor gave up to be invested in the company making $100 per year of profits.

NOW WHAT?

Putting aside the permanent challenge of solving for what future cash flows will be, and how those cash flows have been (or have not been) adequately discounted into the present value, all investing has to solve for the second great question once the first great one has been answered. That first question is whether or not there are profits, but really it is far more complex than that—how sustainable they are, how they will grow, how they can be expanded, which other opportunities exist, how the company will deal with competitive challenges, and on and on. But once we have generally established that a company has real profits and we generally believe that the company will continue to deliver goods and services for a price in excess of the cost of production, the second question is: what will the company do with its profits?

This is what the entire subject of dividend growth investing is about—the decision a profitable company makes about what to do with those profits. It is the heart of the matter. With some investment decisions, one is trying to assess if or when a company may become profitable. In other decisions, one may be trying to assess whether those future profits are appropriately priced in already, and which upside (or downside) surprises might exist. But at the heart of dividend growth investing is the belief that of all the available options for what a company does with its profits, returning a prudent portion of them to investors is the best option.

Some have suggested that a company worth X then pays a dividend, making that company now worth "X-amount of dividend," implying that it is zero-sum. It is certainly true that if a company has $1 billion of cash on its balance sheet and then pays out $500 million of dividends, the company's assets are now down by $500 million. If that company were never to earn profits again—if companies were like "pop-up shops" that came for a weekend, sold a bunch of stuff, and then had money in the bank—any money it pays out lowers the value of the company's bank account. This is not just true, it is insultingly, obviously, true. But it also is a brutal swing and a miss when it comes to how company value is formed. The idea that dividends are just a zero-sum decision around cash in a bank account ("I can have a stock worth twenty or I can have a stock worth nineteen and a dividend worth one") is among the most fallacious critiques I have ever encountered about dividend growth investing.

NOT A ZERO-SUM DECISION

A company is worth the future of its profits, not the sum of the assets on its balance sheet. Granted, those assets matter (such as cash, equipment, notes receivable, intellectual property, licensing rights, royalties, contracts, and real estate), and they factor into the value the market might give to a business. However, the fundamental issue that makes people buy public equities (with the risk and volatility that go therewith) is the belief in future profits above the risk-free rate that the company can or should generate. In the prior example of a company with a billion dollars of cash on its balance sheet paying out $500 million of dividends, one can easily illustrate it as a zero-sum transaction:

Scenario One:
Investors own a company with $1 billion of cash and no dividend coming.

Scenario Two:
Investors own a company with $500 million of cash and $500 million paid to them.

In both scenarios, the value is equal to $1 billion, and the issue is who is holding some or all of that $1 billion.

But that would be illustrating it wrongly, or I should say, incompletely. For all that matters to an investor is where that $1 billion came from, and where the next $1 billion is coming from. In this case, the answer is from *profits,* and so we are not talking about liquidating the company after a pop-up shop weekend. We are talking about what to do with the profits that the company has generated. We do not have a stock worth $20 with no dividend or a stock worth $19 with a $1 dividend, fixed at a point in time, static, and ready for dissolution. No, we have a dynamic business that, after one quarter or year of profits, now has another quarter or year of profits coming, and we have a stock price that has *discounted the expectations of those profits into the price.* The multiple applied to the company's earnings is a reflection of the market's expectation for continued profits, continued profit growth, and sustainability and durability of profits. Obviously, investor sentiment and other macro psychology components affect price, too, but fundamentally, the price of a stock is never merely about the assets on its balance sheet (cash included). The earnings are what matter, and once you understand that profits in the future are the fundamental source of value for a business, you then have a decision to make: what do you want to do with those profits?

WHAT CAN COMPANIES DO WITH PROFITS?

For the sake of simplicity, I am going to suggest the following options for what a company can do with its after-tax profits:

1. It can distribute some or all of those profits to its investors (what we call dividends)
2. It can buy back stock, essentially meaning it has increased value for shareholders by reducing the amount of owners the future profits will belong to.

   For example, a company has a hundred investors with ten shares each and the stock is worth $10/share (for a company value of $10,000). If the company had profits of $1,000 and used it to buy the stock from ten investors, there are now ninety investors with ten shares each, but there is still the same $10,000 of profit, meaning that each of the remaining shareholders owns something worth more than it was before). Essentially, an investor now owns a higher percentage of the same value than he did before because the number of slices in the pie has been reduced!
3. It can use the profits to buy other companies (M&A).
4. It can reduce debt that the company may have on its balance sheet.
5. It can let cash sit on its balance sheet.

6. It can spend the money on new internal projects and expenditures (not outside M&A, but additional ideas, opportunities, inventory, or growth initiatives: reinvestment/capital expenditures).

I suppose there could be other options, but they would almost certainly be subcategories of one of these six major categories. I have devoted my professional life to dividend growth investing and believe enough in the idea of capital return via dividend payments that I am now writing my second book on the subject—but I do not believe dividends represent the only sensible direction for after-tax profits in all cases. There are ample scenarios where all six of the above capital return strategies would be ideal, and each company and each situation has to be evaluated on its own merits.

What I am talking about when I speak to companies optimally managing their own capital allocation with dividends presupposes a certain maturity in the business—where the incremental return on additional projects may be lower than what investors can get elsewhere, or when no such capital is needed for ongoing operations. Many companies reach a maturity where free cash flow productivity is very high—their business model simply does not require heavy reinvestment. High operating cash flow with low capital expenditures equals a high free cash flow that is either going to sit sub-optimally in cash (low yield on cash reserves), going to be invested poorly (the company's core competency—what it does best that generated the free cash flow to begin with—does not require additional capital, so to reinvest into a non-core competency risks malinvestment), or optimally gets returned to shareholders.

WHEN REINVESTMENT MAKES SENSE

There are plenty of companies that do require capital expenditures to keep the profits coming into the future. This does not always make them poor dividend payers or dividend growers, but it does speak to the challenge of adjudicating where reinvestment is needed to protect future profits (and therefore, future dividends).

Airlines and railroads and container shipping companies are pretty permanently "asset-heavy" businesses (and, I should point out, pretty poor dividend growers in most scenarios).

Power plants are very capital-intensive, yet utilities have often been great dividend payers (largely due to their regulated fee business models).

Oil and gas companies are pretty capital intensive (upstream companies need ongoing rigs and drills, while midstream companies need ongoing pipelines), so that even where operating cash flows are attractive, their capital expenditures have to be constantly managed in the grand scheme of the cyclicality of the business.

Automakers are extremely asset-heavy and require extraordinary reinvestment in assembly lines, product innovation, and machinery. They also tend to have high indebtedness, as well as often have expensive labor contracts and benefits, making dividend sustainability a challenge.

REITs have significant capital tied into brick, mortar, and dirt, and if they didn't, they probably wouldn't be REITs. Their growth is not only dependent on generating more cash from the real estate they do own, but also on acquiring new real property (whatever the category may be), meaning that they need to manage their income statement in a way to ensure that adequate reinvestment is given a good priority in their capital allocation.

There is nothing wrong with a company that needs heavy reinvestment, and when the return on assets (net income divided by total assets) is attractive enough, it generally means the company is managing its investments resourcefully.

Other sectors do not require the same degree of reinvestment—mainly because the cost of generating the revenue was an early investment and the ongoing production of goods and services can happen on the strength of technology, a brand, or a platform already in place.

Consumer staples companies usually have limited reinvestment needs once their brands have reached maturity in the marketplace.

Software companies are usually thought of as the ultimate asset-light companies, as adding customers comes with little cost and the operating leverage is substantial.

Asset managers and professional services companies usually have their cost embedded in people and personnel, but not in a heavy capital intensity.

The point here is not to claim that one sector or another has an embedded investment superiority to another, but rather to establish that different companies and sectors have different reinvestment/capex needs. The most enthusiastic of dividend growth investors will always support and defend adequate levels of capital expenditures to ensure ongoing business sustainability.

WHAT ABOUT THAT M&A OPTION?

Excess cash breeds complacency. The testimony of history is abundantly clear. One can say all day that company management is incentivized not to let that happen, but the incentive differentials between management and ownership are an important part of this conversation. A company's board of directors often picks capital return strategies (like dividends) because the alternatives include the company's managers spending too much money, taking bad risks, and, the mother of them all, poorly thought-through mergers and acquisitions.

As Appendix II of this book demonstrates using the media sector as an example, few uses of after-tax profits have set more capital on fire than M&A. This is, of course, not universally true. Many corporate transactions have proved to be very accretive, attractively priced, and strategically beneficial. The prudent dividend growth investor never argues that all M&A is bad—merely that much of it is—and that having a governor in place (like a consistent growing dividend policy) mitigates against the risk of vanity projects and empire building that much corporate M&A represents.

The alleged benefits of M&A are easy enough to understand: Synergies can be created when the revenues of two companies can be combined with something less than the costs of two companies (eliminating certain redundancies in expense). The end result may very well be one company that generates more profits than the two companies put together did as cost efficiencies, pricing power, and the reduction of competition are achieved. That is the easy part.

The hard part is the price paid. Why would Company B sell to Company A for its fair market price when it is already worth the fair market price, meaning that Company A has to pay a *premium* for Company B to entice it, and that premium is the risk to the shareholders of Company A?

But the risk does not end at the price paid, though that is often a big enough risk. The assumed synergies often do not materialize, the company cultures often do not mix well, and the competitive advantages often underperform expectations, leading to significant capital deterioration.

Besides the media sector examples I write about in Appendix II, corporate America is filled with companies that used both after-tax profits and excessive debt to fund ill-gotten mergers M&As which hurt investors immensely. The problems here are not usually because the financial inputs were wrong or the execution was poor, but because the motivations were unaligned with what was best for the shareholders. The egos and pathologies of corporate managers can find M&A attractive, and the ability to use someone else's money to fund these pursuits can be irresistible. But when M&A goes poorly, the shareholders pay the price, and history is filled with examples.

THE MOST POPULAR ALTERNATIVE, SORT OF

Most critics of dividend growth investing would, if they were being intellectually and economically honest, grant all I have said so far in this chapter. A bunch of cash earning the risk-free rate on the balance sheet of the company is a low return for investors. Capital reinvestment needs matter, but must be managed prudently, and, in many cases, no such need exists (without the company varying from its core business in a very ill-advised manner). M&A has its place, but needs to be reined in, prudently pursued, and can be held in check when subjected to a dividend growth commitment that limits delusions of grandiosity.

So, if we are talking about an investment universe of mature, profitable companies (not start-ups, venture, or pre-profit companies), and we understand the various challenges with all the aforementioned deployments of after-tax profits, do dividend payments to shareholders win by default?

The "stock buyback" option continues to be one that many hold onto as a use of profits that allegedly benefits investors more than dividends. Once again, after a deeper look, this simply does not hold up to scrutiny.

Chapter Eight of *The Case for Dividend Growth* was devoted to the case for dividends as a superior form of capital return versus stock buybacks. The chapter has held up well. I would argue, though, that even more intense arguments exist now since that chapter was written eight years ago. I went to great lengths in that chapter to make clear that I am not opposed to stock buybacks—and most certainly not opposed to stock buybacks for the reasons that many now are in the political sphere. The *en vogue* argument from certain progressive groups and even populist "new right" groups that stock buybacks hurt workers and wage-earners is, as far as I am concerned, indefensible. It is a popular class warfare argument, pitting profits (the source of cash from which stock buybacks are funded) against wages. It is not my argument. Mine is entirely rooted in the optimization of investor results as it pertains to the *use of after-tax profits* (which, by definition, means we are talking about after wage-earners have been paid, bonuses paid, and new hires made).

Many proponents of stock buybacks versus dividends argue that these are essentially the same thing, with stock buybacks benefitting from tax treatment and timing flexibility. My response is if they were the same thing, why not give the investors the choice (via dividend reinvestment) if they want the benefit of more ownership (stock buybacks theoretically increase ownership by reducing the share count of other investors; dividend reinvestment gives the investor more shares by increasing their own share count)? It is essentially a stock buyback optionality, but with the option held by the risk-taker—the minority owner of the business—not the corporate manager.

But I am being far too nice in my rebuttal. If the premise were true—that stock buybacks and dividend payments were essentially the same thing to the investor—I would still favor giving the investor the *choice*. But the premise is not true—that investor ownership is increasing from stock buybacks as the reverse dilution of a reduced share count kicks in from stock buybacks over time. All we need to disprove this premise is the utterly empirical fact that nearly every company that has participated in heavy stock buybacks in recent years and decades has far more of a share count now than it did when it started! How is this possible, you ask? Because stock buybacks are not returning cash to shareholders in most cases, but replacing new shares issued by the company in the form of executive compensation.

I need to be clear: There is nothing wrong with companies paying their employees and executives, and there is nothing wrong with doing so with stock options and restricted stock units. But if the cash spent on stock buybacks (cash that comes from after-tax profits) is not leading to a material reduction in share count (and, in fact, is often accompanied by a meaningful *increase* in share count), then you *cannot* call this a return of capital to shareholders. It is not shareholder yield. It is executive compensation. Period.

How do companies get away with this? Well, in many cases, in certain periods, the returns of the sectors doing it have been good enough that investors have not complained. But it also requires a different diligence than other capital return strategies involved. A company announces a dividend, and it has a contractual payment to make to its owners, and that payment is final. An investor can use that payment to buy more shares, but the company has said A-B-C, done A-B-C, and the investor sees A-B-C. It is both simple and transparent.

Not so with stock buybacks! A company announces an "authorization" to buy back shares over a period of time—sometimes over many years. That "buyback program" is not guaranteed, committed, or even executed in any real-time transparency, and when shares are bought back, the investor does not know how many other shares were issued in the same time period. It takes years to be able to really calculate what net shareholder yield was achieved (if any) by the "authorization" of a share buyback program.

Not only are share buybacks not really the alternative to dividends that they are heralded to be, and not only could they exist with *investor optionality* just by letting shareholders *choose* to buy more stock with their dividends (as most accumulators do), but they also are demonstrably less reliable than dividends, even outside the various structural flaws I have already highlighted.

In the 2008–2009 financial crisis, a well-run dividend growth portfolio should have had zero (or very few) dividend cuts. Across the S&P 500, dividends were down by 20 percent, higher than I believe is acceptable, but still pale in comparison to the *90 percent reduction in stock buybacks that took place.* During the COVID-19 market period, buybacks dropped from $1.05 trillion in 2019 to $758 billion in 2020—a drop of 28 percent. While sixty-five S&P 500 companies announced a dividend cut or suspension, the dividend payment drop for the S&P 500 was a whopping 2 percent in 2020 (versus 28 percent reduction in stock buybacks).[2]

There is something far more striking about this than just the crystal-clear demonstration that stock buybacks are not a consistent and sturdy means of returning capital to shareholders. They are also, apparently, the worst-timed and most counterintuitive mechanism in corporate finance! During periods like the global financial crisis, the COVID market swoon, and the 2022 tech crash, when stock prices were, arguably, in a rare period of being cheap and attractive, company treasurers *stop* buying shares, and in periods where shares are much more expensive and valuations are more stretched, companies buy more shares. It is the opposite of what we think of as investor common sense.

WHY THIS MATTERS

All this is not to dunk on stock buybacks (which absolutely have their place), but to make a positive argument about the reality of dividend payments. The simple fact of the matter, embedded in investor expectations, is that the *implicit*

2 Allen He, "How the Pandemic Has Impacted Buybacks," FCLT Global, January 10, 2022, https://www.fcltglobal.org/resource/how-the-pandemic-has-impacted-buybacks/.

promise in dividend payments is that they will be maintained. It is up to us as dividend growth managers to assess if the companies *can do so,* but the "social contract," for lack of a better term, views dividends as far more indispensable than stock buybacks. The message from a dividend cut is never one a company wants to send ("We are in a lot of trouble."), whereas the message from a stock buyback that never happens is, well, often nonexistent, since by the time investors know that authorized shares were not repurchased in a certain distress period, that period has come and gone.

Not only are market signals and market expectations very different between the two capital return strategies, but one appeals to *both* major category of investors—accumulators and withdrawers—where the other appeals *only* to accumulators. You can buy groceries with dividends. You cannot buy anything with stock buybacks. Of course, you can sell shares if you want to buy groceries, but then you own fewer shares—you have minimized the tree from which you want future fruit. If one does not want groceries from one's portfolio, and, in fact, does want more ownership of the company paying the dividends, one can reinvest dividends and accomplish just that. Dividends are a capital return benefit for *both* accumulators *and* withdrawers of capital.

It is empirically undeniable that dividends have proven stickier than stock buybacks for investors and have far more achieved the desired end of returning capital to investors.

THE AGENCY PROBLEM

If there is ever a time that the phrase "giving back" is used correctly, it is when we talk of a company returning capital to shareholders. In that case, investors really did give capital to an enterprise, and when they receive profits from that investment, the company is "giving them back" their money (along with whatever return on that investment it generated—such as a coupon payment for a bondholder, or a share of profits for a stockholder).

Dividends as a means of returning capital to shareholders benefit multiple categories of investors. They align management with the risk-taking owners of the business. They constrain corporate managers from some of their own worst instincts. They can always be done (and almost always are) in conjunction with other uses of after-tax profits (reinvestment, capex, prudent share buybacks, some measured and thoughtful M&A), but when a company has a culture of dividend growth, the social contract and expectation is categorically more investor friendly.

That dividends are a constant de-risking of an investment made while buybacks are a constant re-risking is true enough. Ultimately, how profits are treated speaks to what is known as the principal–agent problem—the embedded conflict that exists between "agents" (corporate managers) who are hired to make decisions on behalf of "principals" (shareholders). This conflict can never be perfectly resolved, but how companies treat their own profits is the ultimate test of the agency problem, and dividends are the ultimate solution.

Dividends force capital market discipline, they put the onus on management to justify capital needs, and they constrain the worst instincts to which corporate managers are susceptible. Using profits to retain capital, reinvest capital, or buy back shares are all expansions of management control. Only dividends move some element of governance and control to the owners of the business. Dividends represent capital discipline in a day and age often known for reckless capital ambition.

Good companies generate profits over time. Investors are wise to put some of those in their pocket. Dividends allow investors to *profit from the profit.*

CHAPTER NINE

PUTTING IT INTO PRACTICE

"The stock market is filled with individuals who know the price of everything, but the value of nothing."
—PHILIP FISHER

THIS WAS THE MOST FUN chapter to write, and you can decide where it ranks in the fun of reading it. As much as I love all the foundational elements we have covered in prior chapters, there is very little I love more than managing dividend growth money. The reasons for it all matter, and were it not for all of the history, arguments, and reasoning in the preceding chapters, I wouldn't be a dividend growth portfolio manager. But now that you understand *why* we believe in this approach to investing, I believe the *what* and the *how* matter. I use this chapter to elaborate on the specifics of security selection and to offer a framework for how the whole management of these selected securities works. I address the question of whether we use covered call-writing to enhance the yield on positions we own (hint: we do not), and I answer the question of where dividend growth fits into a more comprehensive portfolio allocation. I told you this was fun stuff!

THE PROOF IS IN THE PUDDING

It should be a reasonably easy concept to grasp that a dividend growth portfolio is as good as the dividend growth companies that are in it. There is no secret recipe to a portfolio that transcends the sum-of-its-parts math that creates the weighted result. Dividend growth as a governing philosophy requires execution, and the results will be a direct reflection of the companies that are selected. It is a "top-down" philosophy that is managed on a "bottom-up" basis. The high dispersion of results that exists within dividend growth is a direct by-product of how wildly different company selection can be in the actual portfolio management.

It goes without saying that a key feature of a dividend growth stock ought to be a dividend that is growing. Because we want a total portfolio yield that is somewhere around 4 percent (this range has been at or above the ten-year bond yield for most of the past twenty years and has been at or above double the S&P 500 yield for the same), we prefer to buy companies that offer a yield at purchase higher than that of the S&P 500. We can buy a company with a yield of just 2 percent if we believe there is significant dividend growth on the horizon, but if we are to achieve a weighted yield of 4 percent across the whole portfolio, we can only do that sparingly (and with other higher dividend names counterbalancing). But the quantitative and qualitative metrics that go into assessing the dividend growth we can expect from the company, as well as our assessment of its sustainability, are extensive.

It is conventional enough to say that we believe business models which feature recurring and predictable cash flows make for better dividend growers than others. Companies whose profit action is dependent on commodity prices may see fluctuation in profits that call into question the sustainability of the dividend.

The oil and gas sector, though, is a great example of how this has to be considered with nuance. ExxonMobil and Chevron have managed to grow the dividend every single year for many, many decades despite having a large exposure to a very unpredictable and volatile input—the price of oil. Other integrated oil companies have not been so fortunate, experiencing a dividend cut when the commodity cycle turned against them (Shell, British Petroleum, ConocoPhillips, and Occidental). Should we conclude that oil companies are intrinsically more exposed to dividend cuts? Perhaps. But Exxon and Chevron suggest that something else may be at play. First, their own track records speak to empirical support for their commitment to and the resilience of the dividend. Second, many oil companies did not cut their dividend over the years because oil prices went down, but because oil prices went down *and* they were over-levered. Commodity prices matter to companies that sell the underlying commodity, and commodity prices matter to companies that have to buy the commodity as an underlying input. Nearly every company is exposed to the latter to some degree; fewer are exposed to the former. But it takes analysis to determine if the risk is merely the cyclicality of commodity prices, or that dynamic *combined with something else.* Leverage, pricing power, distribution, market share, and yes, history, tell us far more than blanket assertions do.

The airline industry and the automaker industry are also cyclical, have commodity price exposure, and have historically been dividend-vulnerable. But further analysis indicates that those concerns become more contextualized when one understands union labor costs, retiree pension commitments, and, yes, leverage ratios. Not every sector is created equal (consumer staples offer far more dividend durability as a general rule than energy companies), but not all companies within a sector are created equal, either.

Some companies are more recession-proof than others. We refer to more defensive sectors, such as utilities, consumer staples, and health care, versus more cyclical sectors, such as industrials, materials, and financials. Essentially, people still need to pay their electric bills, buy diapers, and get medicine during a recession. Should a dividend growth portfolio be *only* invested in defensive sectors? Of course not! But when a sector has intrinsic challenges in it (such as cyclicality and commodity exposure), one has to be more selective about the debt profile, business model, and, yes, track record, of the company itself.

Even defensive sectors might have currency exposure or input cost exposure. Indeed, even companies in a defensive sector might make a strategic misstep (we have seen plenty!). Sometimes the dividend growth track record—that is, the ability to keep generating free cash flow and to keep growing the dividend paid from such cash flows—through a wide array of periods is the best testimony of earnings resilience. Good businesses still make mistakes, but long-term dividend growers have demonstrated an ability to repair what is wrong and have created a capital structure that gives them the stability they need through either tough times or even operational blunders.

We believe the payout ratio matters, both to indicate a management commitment to the dividend (not too low), but also a margin of safety (not too high). There is more on this point below when we look at the reality of different yield quintiles within the market. There must be flexibility to appreciate companies with extremely high cash flow productivity that have a very safe ability to pay out a high payout ratio because of their own business moat, market share, pricing power, irreplaceable distribution networks, and other structural advantages. I do not want to suggest that any company *ever* has the luxury of complacency, but some companies have higher margins than others. If a company with such a protected position begins to make operational or strategic mistakes, there should be ample time for an astute manager to make adjustments.

At the end of the day, from the company's balance sheet, to its net cash position, to its leverage, to its dividend history, to the quality of its earnings, to any other metric we could study (and we study all of these and more), there is nothing that matters more than *the cultural commitment to the dividend.* A management team that consistently but begrudgingly pays (and grows) the dividend will turn on you when given the chance. Now, a management team that is genuinely committed to the dividend that oversees a broken business will not be able to pay you a dividend either, so strong cultural *propensity* for returning cash to shareholders must come with an *ability* to do so. But even companies that have that ability will find a way to lose it when management is not committed. The trappings of hoarding excessive cash at a subpar return on equity, or worse, doing destructive M&A, are real. In all our endeavors as fundamental analysts at my firm, no challenge is greater as a dividend growth manager than finding those companies for which the dividend and its annual growth is a true part of their cultural commitment.

PASSIVE VERSUS ACTIVE DEBATE

The entire preceding section speaks overwhelmingly to dividend growth as a strategy that requires *active* management. Many of the quantitative criteria can be screened and ascertained passively (such as minimum yield threshold, track record of dividend growth, and dividend payout ratio), but the qualitative assessment of dividend sustainability and cultural propensity around the dividend require judgment and discernment. The reason so many passively managed dividend growth strategies (in the exchange-traded fund [ETF] and mutual fund space) have such low distribution yields or have experienced so many dividend cuts within their own holdings is due to this very lack of active overlay.

Regulatory constraints keep me from touting the dividend growth ETF for which we serve as portfolio manager,[1] so I won't do that here. What I will say is that several things bother me in the universe of passive dividend growth strategies (whether they be ETFs or otherwise):

1. Rules-based approaches measure the past, and cannot measure sustainability. Screens are, by definition, backward-looking, and they provide much vital and

1 The Bahnsen Group, "TBG DIV Focus," http://www.tbgdividendgrowth.com.

relevant information, but there is information they cannot provide—and that information matters. A judgment about whether a business is deteriorating or vulnerable can be fallible, but in dividend growth investing, where your goal must be avoiding dividend cuts, it is vital.

2. Many passive funds overly rebalance on pre-scripted, rules-based formulas that negatively influence the compounding effect and limit the personal yield over time to the investor.
3. Passive strategies often offer a lower yield than an optimal dividend growth strategy should offer, even mirroring or nearing the S&P 500's low yield. This is a by-product of their screening criteria that is agnostic to current yield at purchase and overly relies on backward-looking indicators that may be well-priced into the stock (and consequently, the current yield).
4. Some of the funds flat-out cheat. Rather than take the risk of missing some of the beta available in a strong beta market, they will add names of the tiniest of yields (Nvidia, Meta) just to have the Big Tech/Mag 7/trend *du jour* exposure in the portfolio, no matter how contra-dividend growth philosophy the names may be.
5. Though this seems redundant to point (1) above, the critique is different. Because of what is stated in point (1)—that these passive approaches rely on backward data and lack the ability to filter around quality and conviction—they not only hold inferior names at times, or miss out on superior names, but the

> timing of exit from broken stories becomes sub-optimal. Essentially, they are generally forced by their own rules-criteria to hold names until after they have cut the dividend, not only missing the opportunity to proactively manage around this risk, but inviting the worst of all worlds in exit timing. Passive dividend stock selection combines an inferior selection criteria (relative to an active approach) with an inferior reaction function (the speed of response relative to an active approach).

I could add that not only are rules-based criteria "necessary but not sufficient," but the rules themselves are often ill-advised. A general rule of thumb of wanting to see ten years of consecutive dividend growth is fine, but what about companies that have been public for only four years, or seven years, but will be growing the dividend for the next ten or twenty? An active approach (with its embedded fallibility) allows for future dividend growers, without waiting until they have gotten much more expensive. There are some examples of opportunity cost near the end of this chapter.

WHEN BUY AND HOLD IS FAR TOO RIGID

In Chapter Five, I explained the concept of yield on original investment (YOI). In a nutshell, for a long-term investor buying a successful dividend-growing stock, waking up one day with a yield of 50 percent to 100 percent (the dividend that the investor receives down the line divided by what she paid for the stock at purchase) is not only lovely, but extremely common and achievable. And, as I earlier argued, it should both reinforce how the dividend pulls the stock price higher (current yields don't go to 100 percent, but yields-on-cost do, meaning—because of math—that the stock prices went up!), but also what the benefit is for the accumulator with a future cash flow objective. It is a complete paradigm shift in thinking for those who truly understand it.

That said, many could mistake the YOI aspect of dividend growth investing for a rigid buy-and-hold practice. That need not be the case. It is my contention that few things matter more for a dividend growth manager than a sell discipline. Both in terms of the management of opportunity costs and overall risk management, to argue that dividend growth management requires an active approach implies (by definition) that some sell discipline must be at play. Here is mine:

- If we believe the ownership thesis is broken (the strategic and operational case for the company), selling is the right thing to do. Sometimes, the dividend may still be paid and may even be growing, but in certain very rare cases, what excited an investor at purchase may change categorically. This requires humility and flexibility. In dividend growth investing, I am happy to say that broken ownership theses are also a rarity.
- Most importantly, if we believe the sustainability of the dividend is questionable, selling has to be considered. From new (ill-advised) M&A, to a change in the debt profile and leverage rates, to a new management team that talks down the dividend, to an incremental slowing in free cash flow growth, to a regulatory hurdle or headwind,

to any number of other factors that should cause concern for the future dividend—these catalysts all warrant a sale event for a dividend growth investor.

- While the first two criteria are negatives, the final one is a very positive scenario, and one that happens commonly for good dividend growth investors. That is when a company has executed so well, grown its dividend as hoped (or perhaps even more so), and yet the stock price has escalated at such a higher pace than the dividend that the price gain covers multiple years of expected dividend growth, and allows you to replace that stock with something of better current yield *and* more opportunistic dividend growth. "Accidental high yielders" are when a company's dividend has not changed but its stock price has dropped precipitously. But we can also look at companies that are "accidental low yielders"—companies whose stock price rose so much that their robust dividend growth could not prevent their yield from falling to 1 percent or thereabouts. In recent years, investors have seen this with Broadcom (AVGO), Walmart (WMT), and Apollo (APO), just to name three examples. Sometimes, a name might drop a lot after it is sold for this reason (Apollo), and at other times, it might not. But for the dividend growth investor, there is an opportunity cost to holding an accidental low yielder, especially one whose future dividend growth expectations are subpar to other opportunities.

I do not mind saying that in a perfect world, the perfect time to sell a dividend growth is never. But it is not a perfect world, and the realities of a dynamic marketplace are such that a dividend growth portfolio, even one focused on building a very high YOI, will benefit from an active approach that utilizes both defensive and offensive sell disciplines.

TWO MISTAKES AT BOTH ENDS OF THE SPECTRUM

There are two different things that I run into quite a bit in the world of dividend investing. Polar opposites of one another, they both run afoul of what this book is arguing for in terms of investment strategy.

One is the confusion of high yield stocks for dividend growing stocks, something so common and, often, treacherous that I devoted the last chapter of *The Case for Dividend Growth* to it. The thesis is not that high-yield stocks are bad, but that they *might* be bad, and the objective described in this book is fundamentally about *growth of income,* and how that speaks to a business quality and durability that has proven superior over time. The "might be bad" may not apply to companies that have a high yield because they have a large payout ratio and the distribution divided by stock price results in a superlative yield, but it could very well apply to companies that were $100 stocks paying a $4 dividend (4 percent yield), and are now a $50 stock paying a $4 dividend (8 percent yield). Of course, some of those 50 percent retracement companies could have a story the market fails to appreciate, but these "accidental high yielders" are very often dealing with a fundamental challenge that has to be evaluated.

The other extreme I hear is more forgivable, but also outside the strategy I advocate in this book. That is the "aristocrats" where there is an inadequate attention to yield at purchase. In other words, some would suggest that if the dividend is going to grow year-over-year, buying at a 0.65 percent yield is not a problem. My team and I beg to differ.

I am not suggesting an excessive formulization to address this, and what I am about to say is more of a framework and reinforcement than a quantitative rule. But if our usual approach to the two errors described above is to generally avoid "high yielders" that became such by rational stock price depreciation and to likewise avoid "aristocrats" where the stock price is rich, reflecting the known dividend growth, as evidenced by the low yield, then it stands to reason that the "tails" of the highest-yielding stocks (let's call them first quintile, the top 20 percent of highest-yielding stocks) and the lowest-yielding (for simplicity, let's call these the fourth and fifth quintiles, the bottom 40 percent of yields within the market) may not be the most attractive buckets from which to buy. Further, that the second quintile may serve as a sort of "sweet spot" for dividend growers.

Let's evaluate why this is. First, there are plenty of great companies in the "first quintile" of dividend yield that did not get there as an "accidental high yielder." I want to repeat how this is not a hard-and-fast rule and requires a qualitative and bottom-up assessment. That said, the average dividend payout ratio of first quintile yielders has been 75 percent for most of my lifetime. The average yield for second quintile yielders has been 40 percent. What this indicates is that there is a far greater margin of safety for second-quintile companies than there is for first-quintile companies.

Average Dividend Payout Ratio
(1979-2024)

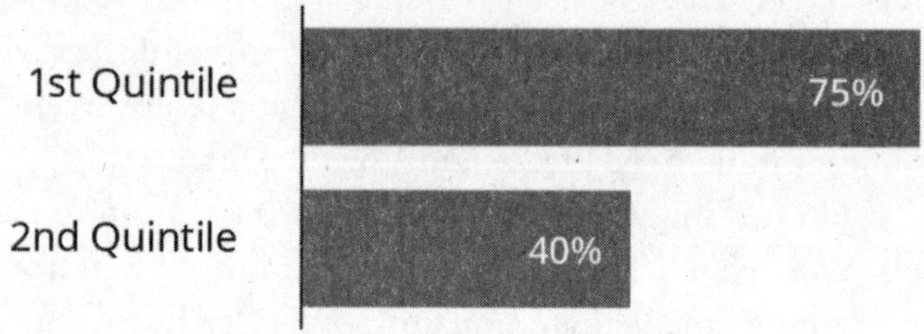

If the earnings of a company paying out 80 percent to 100 percent of earnings were to drop 15 percent to 25 percent, that company is in a mathematical danger zone of either needing to cut the dividend or pay it from the balance sheet (or borrow money to pay it). Some dividend growth companies have the pricing power and predictability of cost structure that a 20 percent earnings drop is truly unlikely. When a company has a historical track record of avoiding those kind of earnings troughs, even in highly distressed events or periods, a higher dividend payout ratio may make a lot of sense (remember that these things are not rigidly formulaic). But as a rule of thumb, the second quintile of dividend payers generally has a generous and rewarding dividend payout ratio that leaves a margin for error. This makes dividend cuts much less frequent and generally indicates a more stable and reliable group.

The performance history bears this out. Here you see that the second-quintile stocks have outperformed the S&P 500 in seven of ten decades going back a century—better than any other grouping. Most notably, you see the lowest yielders lagging behind all other groups.

SECOND-QUINTILE STOCKS OUTPERFORMED MOST OFTEN (1930-2024)

Percentage of Time Dividend Payers by Quintile Outperformed the S&P 500 Index

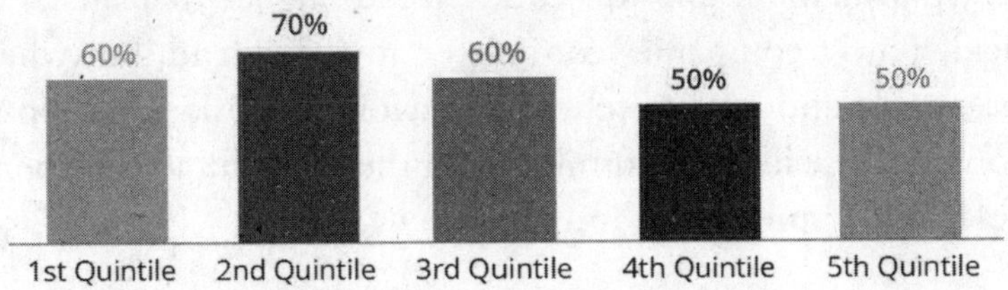

Source: *Hartford Funds, Wellington Management, March 2025

When we look into the weeds of it, we not only see the best relative performance in this grouping, but also a perfect track record of positive performance (something no other quintile can boast, and something the S&P 500, itself, cannot boast).

COMPOUND ANNUAL GROWTH RATE (%) FOR U.S. STOCKS BY DIVIDEND YIELD QUINTILE BY DECADE (1930-2024)

	S&P 500 Index	1st Quintile	2nd Quintile	3rd Quintile	4th Quintile	5th Quintile
Jan 1930 to Dec 1939	-0.20	-2.36	**0.61**	-2.34	-0.38	2.07
Jan 1940 to Dec 1949	9.51	13.92	**13.06**	10.26	8.63	6.83
Jan 1950 to Dec 1959	18.33	18.52	**20.31**	18.47	16.57	19.81
Jan 1960 to Dec 1969	8.26	8.82	**8.90**	6.46	7.97	9.30
Jan 1970 to Dec 1979	6.05	9.67	**10.22**	7.00	7.57	3.94
Jan 1980 to Dec 1989	16.80	20.23	**19.62**	17.20	16.19	14.65
Jan 1990 to Dec 1999	17.96	12.37	**15.54**	15.06	18.10	18.93
Jan 2000 to Dec 2009	-0.44	5.57	**4.15**	4.21	1.99	-1.75
Jan 2010 to Dec 2019	13.65	12.98	**13.25**	14.15	13.68	10.85
Jan 2020 to Dec 2024	14.16	12.04	**10.34**	9.29	16.62	20.19

Source: *Hartford Funds, Wellington Management, March 2025

The point I am making here is not that there is something magical about that second quintile of dividend payers, and not that a rigid formulizing of this concept is a good idea. Rather, it is to use the quantitative data to reinforce the qualitative principle I am advocating: that "higher than market" yields reflect companies committed to a dividend, but when reasonable and not stretched, you avoid the riskiest propositions, and are likely swimming with the most durable, responsible, and impressive swimmers.

COVERED CALLS AND THE MYTH OF FREE MONEY

There was a time when I was asked about once a week why, given my big belief in income-oriented investing, my team and I did not "write covered calls against our dividend growth stocks for yield enhancement." When an investor "writes a call option," it means that he collects a premium from another investor who has bought the call option contract, and has agreed to deliver the stock to him if the stock goes up to the price of the contract. The strike price is generally "out of the money," so you are getting free money if the stock does not go up, and, if it does, you simply deliver the stock (but at that higher price to which it has appreciated). The counterparty to the contract has his own reasons for buying the call option (usually getting leveraged upside for a stock that goes up a lot), but the objective of the person who owns the stock and takes the other side of the contract (the one "writing" the "call option") is the income that comes from these contract premiums.

There are few things that contradict the ethos of dividend growth investing more than covered-call writing.

As this entire book tries to argue, the thesis behind dividend growth investing is owning businesses with tremendous earnings growth that believe in sharing those profits with you in the form of dividends. It has a cyclicality to it throughout the journey of dividend growth equity ownership—there are periods of multiple expansion and multiple contraction, unexpected periods of good sentiment and bad sentiment, and all sorts of fundamental twists and turns. Covered-call writing gives you *small premiums*, but only if you agree to lose *significant upside opportunity*. And, for dividend growth investors, that upside opportunity is the basis of the *compounding* we are after. If a stock does increase to the price in the call option you write, you lose the stock. Yes, you lose it at a premium, but you lost ownership of a company that you did not otherwise want to lose. And you did it all for no reason, or, at least, for a stupid reason—that you were betting on the volatility of the stock staying low. First, how would you know such a thing? Second, why would you care? This approach defies the philosophy of being invested in human action, not market mechanics that are entirely unpredictable. But it comes at a significant cost.

It also changes your portfolio. A dividend growth investor has gone "long" in a great business. A covered-call writer has gone "short" in volatility (and if you really want to get complicated, has gone short in upside convexity). The nature of the portfolio is now less focused on equity ownership, benefitting from the earnings and cash flows and shared profits from great businesses, and more focused on the timing of unpredictable volatile events. It de-emphasizes dividend compounding and invites asymmetrical risk-reward trade-offs that undermine the objective of dividend growth investing.

Allowing your capital to compound without interruption is at the heart of benefitting from dividend growth investing. Covered calls introduce the interruption of this compounding with a very serious tax friction, a stress on timing, and ongoing decisions about rebuying (or not). The income it generates is taxed as *short-term gains* (so, it takes a tax-efficient strategy and couples it with a tax-inefficient strategy), and having stock get called away triggers undesirable capital gains, as well. How do I know they are undesirable? Because if you *desired* them, you would do it on your own—you can always sell a stock at a certain price if you wanted to! These stocks are being sold away because you were hoping to not sell it and just collect the free premium. The more you do this and the more frequent your expiration dates on these contracts, the more likely your delivery of stock (if strike prices are being hit) are happening as short-term capital gains too.

Here is a simple way to think about dividend growth investing: It owns and accepts volatility, and exploits it via dividend reinvestment. Covered-call writing seeks to make money on volatility (or others' expectations of volatility) if it is low, trading the long-term equity premium dividend growth that investors want for the short-term option premium that this strategy entails. No, thank you.

A BALANCED MEAL

For a guy writing his second book on dividend growth investing, I may surprise many of you when I say that I firmly believe in the process of what is called "asset allocation" in a portfolio. In fact, I even believe (vigorously) in something called "alternative investments" (with enough caveats to warrant another book). Allow me to explain our approach to a total portfolio construction.

As mentioned in the Introduction, asset allocation is a necessary part of portfolio construction, not because I believe there is a magic spot where return gets elevated and volatility gets reduced, but because the comfort levels of each investor—their own psychological and emotional dynamics wrapped up in their income needs, liquidity needs, and broader economic considerations—matter. The desired portfolio return of dividend growth (or any equity strategy) requires the investor to own the thing generating the return, and, therefore, an asset allocation that serves the purpose of maintaining ownership, versus facilitating emotional portfolio abandonment decisions, is a good and healthy thing.

So, the most important reason to take seriously the idea of asset allocation is because some investors have a different appetite for volatility than others do. These comfort levels should be informed by reality, but it is not realistic for all humans to sit at peace with the same things. We all have different responses to all sorts of stimuli in life, and there is no reason to believe investment activity would be any different.

There are other reasons to value asset allocation and various elements of customization too. Some investors have different timelines—needs for liquidity—than others. This has to flow from a planning process. A permanent need of *periodic income* is a different objective than the need for certain *lump sum withdrawals*. I take the uncertainty of market volatility so seriously (as well as the history of unexpected drawdown events) that I never like to see money allocated to equities where principal is needed within two years (and I could argue that two years is on the low side of this consideration). Because some investors have high marginal tax rates and some don't, it is wise to address the total tax treatment of the portfolio in the asset allocation (for example, tax-free versus taxable bonds in taxable accounts after considering the tax bracket and state residency of the investor). Some investment goals may require a higher withdrawal rate than the portfolio can comfortably afford, so various "income enhancement" strategies are needed to boost income (to avoid touching portfolio principal).

The bottom line on asset allocation: while I believe the income, the growth, and the growth of the income make dividend growth equity investing a very core position for most asset allocations, there are all sorts of reasons why an investor needs to "asset allocate" to manage the behavioral and emotional dynamics, and other financial objectives the investor may have.

Alternatives are a subset of the asset allocation story. I view the asset class as part of that "volatility" management whereby an investor addresses the *expected volatility of public equities* by replacing that risk with something of *an alternative correlation.* In other words, for the investment to be worthy of the name "alternative," it needs to have a different source of risk and a different source of reward than that which drives public equity (beta) and that which drives public debt (interest rates). The intent is never to "lower" risk but to "change" it. Diversification is at the heart of proper alternative investing, which I have to say is categorically different than how the industry markets itself.

Alternative investments are not a magic potion (high-reward, low-risk), and they are not a return enhancement—they are a risk mitigation (when used properly, that is). Various alternative investments presented as magic sauce that simply use leverage to juice returns are outside of how we want to use them.

When I think about private equity, I am thinking about the same thing I think about with public equities—companies with great operational and strategic direction led by resourceful human beings, seeking to create profits by creating value. That value creation is illiquid in private equity for a time, and can't come back to me through dividends, so it has a different risk/reward paradigm than public equity, but the source of return is the same: human enterprise.

The alternative investment world requires vast due diligence, portfolio monitoring, and will mostly succeed or fail around manager and strategy selection (versus the underlying "beta" of the asset class, which is the driver of returns for public equity index investors). Complementing a dividend growth equity portfolio with alternative investments, when done correctly, can optimize the desired outcome an investor is looking for.

THE HIGHLIGHTS AND LOWLIGHTS

Over the years, we have seen some extraordinary success stories in our dividend growth management, both in terms of what we have *avoided*, and what we have *obtained*. But the world of dividend growth is no exception to the universal law of investing, so you should either enter it with humility, or humility will find you.

In 2007, the decision to sell Citigroup at $50 (split-adjusted, $500) as the company swore it was maintaining the dividend despite borrowing massive amounts of money at very high coupons from Middle Eastern rescue investors was an all-time prescient decision. The inevitable dividend elimination the next year was one problem, but so was the 99 percent drop in the stock that took place through the financial crisis (it is now only down 77 percent, eighteen years later). The issue here was not the avoidance of a stock collapse—it was the use of the dividend and free cash flow/balance sheet/reality around it all, to discern investment truth. Citigroup did not become a broken company because it cut the dividend; it cut the dividend because it was a broken company. Watching a company pay a dividend from free cash flow and then begin a web of balance sheet atrocities that destroyed the company reinforced how *fundamentally* important these things are.

Citigroup is not alone in attempting to use financial parlor games to hide the truth of its business. Accounting mechanisms not only allow it, but sometimes require it. It need not be sinister; it just is what it is. Goodwill and intangibles and special purpose vehicles and amortization schedules are often legitimate and necessary. A company with huge earnings growth that loses cash every year is not only common, but inevitable. EBITDA stands for "earnings before interest, taxes, depreciation, and amortization," meaning the earnings before companies factor in what they pay for debt, and every company today uses debt (with very few exceptions). It can be an accounting scandal like Enron or WorldCom, but it can also just be a textbook case of valuation being completely unhinged from the actual financial position of the company

(AOL in 2000, Citigroup in 2007). It can also be a case of a great dividend payer and grower like AT&T deciding to not be AT&T anymore—to over-lever itself with a terrible acquisition of DirecTV, and then a capital-destroying, culturally incompatible acquisition of Time Warner. Selling that stock in 2018 was not quite the money saver that selling Citigroup was, but believing that excessive leverage and bad M&A undermines dividend sustainability, that sell decision was validated just one year later when a company with more debt than most countries have did exactly what we feared—cut the dividend. And the stock price followed suit.

You have seen charts in this book of companies that have had plenty of up-and-down experiences in stock price over the years but managed to maintain an operating cash flow and a dividend payout that stabilized things for investors. When looking at a company like Blackstone, where The Bahnsen Group presently enjoys a 30 percent YOI, we see a story of pure cash flow growth from a fee-based business that we understood. The stock is up 10x since we bought it, yet it has been down a lot over the past year (at least, as of the time this manuscript was completed). Yet, our YOI has continued growing, and we pray for ongoing volatility, believing in the long-term story of the company.

Dividend growth investors will have success stories like selling Citigroup or AT&T and they will have success stories like buying Blackstone. They will have success stories like owning McDonald's, Procter & Gamble, Johnson & Johnson, and Chevron for decades. But they will also misread the cyclical pressures that can hit a commodity-sensitive business like LyondellBasell. Markets are dynamic and complex. I am very pleased with our track record of buying great dividend growth companies, and equally pleased with our track record of exiting vulnerable positions before they went down the dividend-cut death spiral. But I have made plenty of mistakes, too, or at least been caught offside in my analysis.

The beauty of a diversified, well-managed dividend growth portfolio is that one company running into trouble should never impede the real annual objective of such a portfolio: dividend growth, year-over-year, no matter what is happening with stock market prices and sentiment, and no matter what challenges one or two companies within the portfolio may be encountering.

Humility combined with conviction. Practicality that matters.

CHAPTER TEN

DIVIDEND GROWTH AND DOOMSDAYISM

"I have seen many crises. I have seen many people who were convinced that the end of the world was near. It never was."
—Charlie Munger

"The end of the world is always a very profitable business for those who sell the maps of how to avoid it."
—Unknown

"Pessimism sounds smart. Optimism pays off."
—Naval Ravikant

IT STANDS TO REASON THAT all of my arguments about dividend growth investing, about "profiting from profits," presupposes the continued existence of civilization. Not only would a society where everyone has become extinct be a difficult landscape for dividend growth investing, but it would also create challenges for enjoying one's dividends, as well. Indeed, most of the worst-case scenarios one hears from a certain "doom and gloom" sociological class have always seemed less problematic to me for their investing outlooks than for what one does in that society even if one's investment portfolios were doing well.

But I digress. There are certain "doomsday" forecasts for the world that suggest the public stock market will evaporate (or at least drop in value substantially), that sovereign debt markets will implode, and that the benefits of an economically advanced society will disappear. Of course, there are various gradations of these ideas, and I would be a little unfair to paint all with the same brush. But that said, there is a sociological inclination toward various aspects of deep pessimism that permeates many investors. I say "sociological" because, having spent much of my life with people who meet this description, I have never found this inclination to be ideological. While a certain psychological disposition can lead to ideas which help to rationalize a conclusion, I believe that perma-bearism, doomsdayism, and a general pathological inclination to believe in some catastrophic event is usually about one's emotional wiring and not a coherent view of the world—and certainly not a coherent view of history.

I want to bring this back to dividend growth investing, but first need to make a very important distinction. While I will spend some time here criticizing the world of perma-bearism and doomsdayism (whether it is the opportunistic/grifter type or the entrenched sociological type), this is not the same as believing that "black swan" events can't happen, or that recessions don't happen, or that geopolitical disasters don't happen, or that bear markets don't happen. Like Charlie Munger's quotation at the top of this chapter, I believe in crises, both because I understand human nature and human history, and because I have lived through them and studied them; but I have found the end of the world to be elusive. I can't do much about the con artists who prey on people's fears to generate clicks and subscriptions and to sell books. I can, though, do my level best to protect real people and real investors from the black hole of doomsdayism.

Belief in various crises is a necessary part of believing in the premium returns that exist in risk assets, as well. A world without a left tail on the risk curve is a world with a very shallow opportunity for return on the other side. But my understanding of the world and where we sit on this side of glory finds wars, geopolitical disruption, military conflict, fiscal excess, and a wide array of troubling conditions to be the rule, not the exception. In my adult life managing money, I have seen the multitrillion-dollar implosion of a technology bubble, 9/11, the global financial crisis, the European sovereign debt crisis, the COVID-19 pandemic, and plenty of "smaller crises" that pale in comparison, but, in their own right, warranted attention. The global financial crisis stands out on that list for its relevance to financial markets. Credit, equity, commodities, and real estate were all pummeled, and the collapse of financial assets was part of a broader debacle in the real economy where jobs and wages and corporate profits collapsed, as well. That one seemed to pull out most of the "I told you so" permabears, who, in each such historical moment, prove the old adage about a "broken clock being right twice a day."

Of course, I would argue that the entire list argues for my view of the world more than the doomsday crowd—all risk assets have meaningfully rallied and performed on the other side of those events, and, as fate would have it, those who didn't panic in those moments proved to be the winners; those who did proved to be the victims of the challenges those moments created. But no sane person should minimize the drama, challenge, fear, and damage of the more significant crises we suffer through from time to time (as investors, and also as human beings). My opposition to doomsdayism does not come from a disbelief in crises but an embrace of crises. It comes from a belief that investing for good outcomes does not become fatal in times of crisis; but investing for the outcomes of Armageddon does become fatal in the (highly likely) event that Armageddon does not happen.

One of the tragedies of the doomsday worldview is that it perpetually overstates the risk of the world ending, and perpetually misses the risks that have a 70 to 80 percent chance of happening. Like a neighbor in a burglary-susceptible neighborhood who is obsessed with nuclear war, too many people are making (completely laughable) preparations for what will likely not happen, while having stuff stolen right out of their houses in broad daylight. The proportionality is off. It is time to restore an investing mindset to the base case, not the Armageddon case, and to understand the opportunity costs of failure to do so.

I see periodic bear markets as highly likely. I see "politically acceptable" inflation, but not hyperinflation, as highly likely. I believe downward pressure on postwar trendline real GDP growth to be highly likely. I believe periods of significant valuation excess followed by painful repricing to be inevitable. And I believe the odds of multiyear range-bound markets to be very high when followed by abnormally long secular bull markets.

I can't prove that any of these things will happen. I can't time when they will happen. But I believe that each and every one of them is a high probability event, and, in some cases, practically assured.

So, I ask you, as an investor, what seems more rational? Investing with some plan for the events that have an 80 to 95 percent chance of happening, but without the gift of prophetic timing? Or, investing for events that have a 1 to 5 percent chance (and if you want to say 20 percent, be my guest), but have never happened before, and if they did, leave almost any investment plan obsolete? At the farthest end of left-tail risk events, I do not think enough bearish investors have actually thought through counter-party risk. Let me put it this way: good luck collecting.

But back to the high-probability bad things listed above: some inflation that erodes purchasing power by half every thirty to forty years; range-bound markets where index investors see flat returns every now and then for five to ten years; an economy growing at 1 to 2 percent net of inflation instead of the 3 percent we are used to; asset bubbles bursting; new asset bubbles reflating.

Does any of this sound familiar?

My friends, these are not pulled from the greatest hits of doomsday books and permabear newsletters; they are the real-life conditions we have all been in for a few decades. There have been extraordinary periods in the market (1995–1999, 2003–2007, 2009–2021, 2023–2025) and there have been true challenges (2000–2002, 2008–2009). There have been range-bound markets that people thought the '80s and '90s had left in the rearview mirror (2000–2009). By the time this book comes out, we may be looking at the November 2021 level in the market through 2026 to be a very tepid range-bound period, itself (with a big drop in 2022 followed by big rallies in 2023–2025, followed by a 2026 that rounds it out less than spectacularly). We shall see.

My point is that there are known challenges and the inevitability of real crises, and then there is trying to invest for the end of the world. My belief is that *nothing* prepares for the latter, and that dividend growth prepares for the former. Indeed, the list in the preceding paragraphs (politically acceptable inflation that still erodes purchasing power, range-bound markets, and intermittent crises) was tailor-made for the defensive characteristics of dividend growth investing (for withdrawers), as well as the offensive characteristics (for accumulators).

I learned a long time ago that I will not argue people out of believing in the end of the world. I also learned that someone who is arguing about his asset allocation, while arguing that a collapse of civilization is near, does not believe it himself. If you believe any asset is going to sustain you, or any investment position is going to be honored enough to protect or reward you, then you believe in a milder collapse than you may be letting on.

And while I may not be able to argue people out of a doomsday worldview, I can do my best to convince "normies" of this: Dividend growth investing isn't perfect, and it isn't immune to the reality of the inevitable volatility that comes with pursuit of risk premia. But if you can accept that what you need more than an antidote to nuclear war is an antidote to painful battles, you have found the best solution I have encountered in dividend growth investing. If you can accept that the right solution to concern over getting murdered is to not commit suicide, you may be ready for dividend growth investing.

Profiting from the profit believes in a future that is realistic, but not Pollyannaish. It does not cut off the existence of crises, but nor does it assume that the world will experience no strain. It accepts the constrained vision of the world, yet maintains the historical optimism that can best be described as realism for those who read.

Recessions, wars, pandemics, and financial crises are not hypothetical events. They have happened. They will continue to happen.

And, as they have before and will continue to still, a particular group of companies will continue growing dividends through it all. And each time you receive a dividend in one of those bad periods, you will be reminded that the sun is still rising and setting, that troubles end and opportunities surface, and that the underlying stability of a portfolio that continues to pay you in such periods is an underlying stability of staying power.

Dividend growth investing is not the right strategy for those who believe the end of the world is around the corner. But for those who desire the prudence often missing from today's HODL crowd and those who want to eschew the pessimism of today's doom-and-gloom crowd, you have found a home in dividend growth investing.

CONCLUSION

THE DIVIDEND GROWTH MENTALITY

"The big money is not in the buying and selling, but in the waiting."

—Charlie Munger

DIVIDEND GROWTH IS, AFTER ALL, the very end to which we work.

FIRST AND, PERHAPS, FOREMOST

One of the things I wish I reiterated more about dividend growth investing is the mentality change it *ought* to accompany. This is not to say it always does in the mind of the investor. But from the vantage point of the investment managers (that is, us) it certainly does, and for investors/clients capturing the full essence of its overwhelming benefits, it behooves them to adopt this mentality difference.

What is the mentality of which I speak? It is to concern oneself (at least, primarily) more with the income the portfolio is creating than with the resale value of the holdings at a point in time.

If the resale value is up at a point in time and you are not selling everything to pay legal bills or hospital bills or pay off a bookie or buy a boat, that resale value is, shall we say, immaterial.

If the organic income growth of the portfolio is suffering, disrupted, or broken, you should be concerned. If it is suffering while the resale value is up, *you should still be concerned.* That is counterintuitive for many people. Dividend growth investors need to have their intuitions aligned with logic, reason, and self-interest. And, in this case, dividend income going the wrong way while prices go up is bad.

But of course, the idea of a dividend growth portfolio is that the income *not* go down. Dividends should be increasing if the objective of the portfolio is dividend *growth.* So, if the advisable mentality for a dividend growth investor is to not be happy when resale prices go up despite dividends going down, what is the implied logic when inversed? Resale values also do not matter when they are declining, as long as no immediate liquidation for paying off a kidnapping ransom is required, and when dividends are growing, one should be quite happy (provided they are growing sustainably and at the desired pace).

COUNTING CHICKENS BEFORE THEY HATCH

This is more than just a "don't worry about market volatility" point. That is reasonably good advice for any long-term investor. But this is actually a very important point about the actual investment strategy that has been adopted: Resale prices in public equities go up and down for a whole lot of reasons in the short term unrelated to reality, disconnected from company fundamentals, and immaterial to your objectives as an investor. Long-term, prices reflect the discounted benefits of cash flows you will receive. If the cash flows are coming, growing, and real, the prices will follow. The up-and-down prices (yes, both above and below the line of discounted cash flow reality) on a day-to-day basis are *noise*. The dividends are reality.

Let's try some analogies. Lakers fans should not get excited when LeBron James puts his jersey on; they should be excited when he scores (and appears to be healthy and in a good rhythm on the court). Voters should not be excited when their candidate is polling well eighteen months before an election; they should be excited when the candidate wins the election. The point is that, in a perfect world, all prices reflected in public equities are supposed to be future expectations of cash flows. We know it does not work that way in the short term—sometimes they reflect the fact that a large ETF sold a huge block of stock to meet a redemption for a client who lost a gambling bet, and sometimes they reflect a twenty-three-year-old with a Robinhood account who is showing off for friends by buying high on his app.

TWO CHOICES

Prices matter when you need to sell, but along the way, dividend growth investors know that everything they are doing is centered around the generation of sustainably growing cash flows. Therefore, they have two choices:

1. Focus on what things center around, what matters, what they themselves care about, what they are actually after—the generation of sustainably growing cash flows, or
2. Focus on what cannot be controlled, cannot be anticipated, cannot be known, and cannot be analyzed rationally or coherently—such as short-term price movements.

The mentality of the former ought to be our focus. The mentality of the latter too often is.

THE BUSINESS OF BUSINESS

I intensified my appreciation for dividend growth investing when I more intellectually embraced the distortions that public market reality was creating. At the end of the day, companies in public markets have stock prices and those stock prices trade, often hundreds of millions of shares per day, but they are *companies*, not stock. They are real businesses. Good things happen for the business each day, or maybe bad things do some days, but the stock price does not reflect those things second by second because it often doesn't even know about them. Likewise, I own a business—and things happen some days that are good and other days that are bad. But never in my wildest dreams would I think, "Oh no, XYZ happened today, and if I were to run out and sell my business in the next five minutes, it might be worth a tad less." Likewise, I have never thought, "A-B-C just happened, and it is good, and that means the business is worth more." Things happen to every business, every day, that can influence cash flows, and good operators are running improving businesses and bad operators might be running deteriorating businesses, but why in the world would we think of these things in the context of resale value?

The fact that public market equities provide unfathomable liquidity does not change the fact that we own a business, and the health of that business is reflected in its cash flows over time. Period. We know this with private businesses and act like it isn't true with public ones. The dividend growth mentality fosters more enlightened focus.

WHAT DO I LOSE?

If my point here were to say, "Over time, your portfolio will do worse than alternative ways of investing, but with dividend growth, you don't have to care about it," that would be one thing. But that is absolutely not what I am saying. In reality, the dividend growers have performed better than the entire market in every long-term period I have ever analyzed and have done so with less portfolio volatility. I have no idea what price movement will be for the index in the years ahead or for dividend growers. I do know that the mentality we have not only doesn't know nor forecast, but it also doesn't care.

And that has never come at a cost over the long-term, using history as a guide. Of course, past performance does not guarantee future results.

FRINGE BENEFITS

If all I ever got out of dividend growth investing was a superlative future income that grew over time, I would be very happy. I get a few other things, though, that have to be included in the story:

1. I get more income than just the income produced by what I initially bought. I get that income buying more of that which produces the income (dividend reinvestment) between now and when I need the income so that when I take the income, it will be higher than that generated by my initial investment because I compounded my way to a higher base of income production. (Think of it like using rent checks from tenants to buy more apartment buildings, meaning you get more apartment buildings providing more rent checks.)
2. I get a tax rate that is less than half of the ordinary income rate and identical to the long-term capital gain tax rate.
3. I get a strong tendency for management to operate the company to responsible financial metrics, avoiding the M&A, expenses, and debt levels that routinely bring down otherwise good companies.

4. I get an investment that compensates me for the risk I have taken to be an investor every ninety days, not at some to-be-determined date in the future. In other words, I modestly de-risk every quarter.
5. If I were taking income from the investments (as roughly half of clients do), I would get to insulate my withdrawals from the impact of market volatility, providing a market-price-level-agnostic way of monetizing my investment.
6. I get to give myself a raise every year as income grows year-over-year. I will add that it is not "fixed" income, which is incredibly impressive truth-in-advertising.
7. I get a strategy that, historically, in the most severe moments of distress, has not exacerbated panic at the same level that broad markets have.
8. I get valuations that do not reflect excessive momentum, froth, euphoria, and speculation, but a category of investments that is generally priced in a stratosphere of reason and sense.

What I get, dear reader, is to profit from the profit that makes a market economy go. Nothing could be more fruitful, coherent, or consistent with my philosophy of life than to profit from the profit.

APPENDIX I

THE THEOLOGICAL CASE FOR YIELD THAT GROWS

I WILL CUT TO THE chase. I am well aware that the Bible does not prescribe a specific, literal, detailed investment approach, let alone one as particular as dividend growth investing. The purpose of this appendix is not to say (as I often hear professing Christians in the investment field do) that my exact approach to investing is normatively required in Scripture, nor is it to say that anything other than my approach is normatively prohibited in Scripture. I do not believe either to be true. I am a professing Christian, and I believe that the Bible speaks to all domains of life. As I mentioned in Chapter One, I do believe that all people have a worldview—something that makes up their view of reality, knowledge, and ethics. Mine is rooted in the revelation of God and His Word. And in this revelation, I believe we find principles and truths that are relevant to investing, even if the details of application are not normatively declared. To the extent anyone reads this appendix as saying, "My view of investing is especially biblical, and yours is not," you have read it wrong. But if you read this appendix and find some high-level biblical and creational tenets that deepen your understanding of these things, whether in foundation or application, I will be happy.

I said at the beginning of the book that dividends to investors come from the profits companies make, and that profit comes because human beings are made by God to do profitable things. Dividend growth investors profit from the profit, because they were made by God to be fruitful, multiply, and fill the Earth. We as investors have needs, goals, and wants, and financial markets are a tool through which we find solutions to achieve those goals. But at the same time, those financial markets *would not meet the needs of investors* if the underlying elements of those financial markets *were not first meeting the needs of others*. Company A may pay a dividend to Investor A by which that investor pays for a vacation with her grandchildren, but that dividend can only be paid if Company A first made a product or service that Customer A benefitted from. So, Investor A is rewarded, but only after Customer A is rewarded. In this case, the company is creating yield for multiple parties (the investor and the customer, but very likely the employees, vendors, and other economic actors too). We are used to focusing on the last part of all this as wealth advisors—where it ends up benefitting investors toward their own financial goals and objectives, but we miss much of the beauty and reality if we ever lose track of what is actually happening: value creation that generates a yield.

My contention is that this initial step in the process, the first domino, the *sine qua non* of everything—value creation that generates a yield—is part of the human creativity that was established with *imago Dei*. When God made mankind in His image and likeness, He made us to be co-creators with Him, to solve problems, develop solutions, and blend human effort and ingenuity with the raw materials of the Earth. The "fruit" of this creative process is the value we create, and when it is seen in the light of a capitalized economy, it can be measured with profits. Profits are not the only fruit of our endeavors, and they are not the only way to measure them. Service to others, care and compassion, relational developments, the experiences that happen in our journey—there is far more to this than merely the components that can be measured in profits. But profits are not excluded. They are a part of being fruitful, multiplying, and filling the Earth. These contain strong advocacy of profitable activities, even as the scope of "profitable" there is vastly wider than that which is financial.

What I describe as *imago Dei* was established on the sixth day of Creation. This was the "very good" apex and conclusion that transcended the "good" results of prior days. But the "yield-oriented" nature of Creation did not begin with mankind on day six. The elevated dignity of being a co-creator made to produce and cultivate the Earth was established with mankind, and both the capacity for and commandment to "generate yield" was given to mankind. But the very Earth itself was made for productivity, abundance, and yes, yield. The plants were created with "seeds in themselves"—not a capacity for reproduction but a capacity for "self-replicating abundance."[1] In the raw materials of the world, we have productivity that is compounding, a creation that is designed to multiply over time. While only God is infinite, the immeasurability of Creation's growth potential exceeds our ability to calculate and understand it. We err to believe that dynamism began with the creation of mankind. God made an unfinished world—a good one, but an unfinished one—and He created a world that creates things, itself. In the created world, we have what Jerry Bowyer has called "generative abundance."

I speak of dividend reinvestment (back to financial jargon) as "compounding within compounding"—shares that grow in price, paying out more shares that then themselves generate more shares, which generates more income, and so on. This is essentially the reality of Creation—a compounding created world that is then brought to mankind to compound that which is compounding. Humanity was created to generate and produce in a system that was already generative and productive. This process of cultivation accounts for scarcity and transforms it into abundance. In taking the self-replicating elements of creation and ordering them, cultivating them, and extracting value from them, mankind *enhances* yield. It is not *creating* yield; it is exponentially adding to the yield that was already there. And it is the purpose of humanity, to steward Creation toward the purpose of dividends (and again, that has a very non-financial context here).

---

1 I remain eternally grateful to my dear friend and partner, and renowned Christian economic thinker, Jerry Bowyer, for his teaching on this subject. As has frequently been the case in my relationship with Jerry, I have taken scriptural understandings and teachings and believed I had fully extracted the needed messages from them, especially when it came to economics. Then Jerry comes along with an even vaster and more illuminating perspective, and adds to the depth of my understanding all over again.

Our stewardship of the world God made leads to markets. It leads to mankind interacting together in a way that offers direction, purpose, and growth. Economic advancement has never been accidental. Indeed, it was embedded in Creation.

Aristotle once argued that money is barren. He is certainly right that coins and bills do not reproduce themselves. How, then, does interest come from money? How do dividends come out of stocks? What Aristotle missed was that money and capital are not the same thing. The duplicative, multiplicative, exponential, creative, productive thing is never currency, never a medium of exchange, and never a raw material or commodity. Capital is not money. The creational element of human beings is what "capitalizes money." Yield does not come from currency; it comes from the creative work of mankind. That is the source of capital growth—of return on investment. And financial yield is impossible apart from the yield of creation. Money does not grow; wealth grows—meaning, the goods and services that come from economic work, risk-taking, and productive endeavor.

This is the story of yield. And it is not a financial story, but a creational one.

Investors do not need to reduce their strategy or process to "speculation" because our story is one of nonspeculative stewardship. We will make mistakes, err in judgment, and lose out to competitors. But we are not trying to take a higher piece of a zero-sum world as investors; we are trying to capture the fruits of efforts to grow the world, to generate growth through responsible management and cultivation.

The dividend is a metaphor *and* a literal receipt of this creative process. It constrains the worst tendencies of corporate managers, but it also serves as a guide, reminder, and reward for the investor. For investors, it is an *ownership benefit* that speaks to participation in productivity. That there ought to be benefits to ownership is a core tenet of biblical economics.

Dividend growth investing stems from productive activity and allows capital to be redeployed in service of real productive enterprise. It is the antithesis of investment strategies that argue for capturing something from someone else. The returns do not come from a "one winner, one loser" approach, but from "new winnings."

Those "new winnings" are the by-product of the work of mankind, made in the image of God. That yield rewards investors. And that yield is the end to which we work. And this is all true in so many ways that it leaves me with abundant joy.

APPENDIX II

MEDIA SECTOR PATHOLOGIES THAT PROVE THE POINT

THIS TEXT ORIGINALLY APPEARED IN Dividend Cafe *on January 16, 2026. It seemed appropriate to reprint here, with edits and modifications as needed.*

At the time this very manuscript was written, the household name, Netflix, announced plans to acquire the household name, Warner Bros. This came a couple of months after the household name, Paramount, announced its own pursuit of Warner Brothers, and that came a month after the not-quite-household-name, Skydance, closed its deal to buy Paramount. The entity known as Paramount was really the combined household names of Paramount, Viacom, and CBS.

As corporate skullduggery goes, it has been a pretty exciting ride, and by the time this book has gotten to your hands, who knows what other turns the story may have taken? As much as I love market history and corporate drama as a matter of intellectual curiosity and business chronicles, what animates me most in these merger sagas are the investment lessons. I want to suggest that the history of mergers and acquisitions in the media sector is one giant lesson about dividend growth investing.

The history of Paramount is a fascinating story no matter what your interest in investing may be. And, no matter what happens with Skydance's quest (remember, Skydance now owns Paramount) to nudge Warner Bros. away from Netflix, there are decades of action in the Paramount story that speak to one of the most significant lessons I have learned as a dividend growth investor. Whether it be in the twenty-five years I have practiced dividend growth investing, or in the decades-long study to which I have devoted myself, I believe history provides ample reinforcement of some basic realities of capital allocation. If you ever need to be reminded of why a company's approach to capital return for its investors matters, look no further than the media and content sector.

In today's *Dividend Cafe*, we look to history as a guide, and some "household" names that have managed to set billions upon billions of dollars on fire despite their stewardship of some of the most iconic brands and media properties in world history. At the end of the day, not only do profits matter, but what a company does with them, as well.

WHEN DESTROYING CAPITAL RUNS IN THE FAMILY

It wasn't one of the most heavily trafficked issues of *Dividend Cafe* last year, but one of my personal favorites (as the writer) was my reflection on the AOL–Time Warner merger of twenty-five years prior.[1] I specifically, and quite literally, referred to it as "the worst business deal in history." The staggering stupidity, arrogance, recklessness, and delusion that went into that deal are no less stunning to read about today than they were in the immediate aftermath a generation ago.

PAST IS PROLOGUE

Though I am going to be focusing more on the company formerly known as Paramount, the aforementioned AOL–Time Warner is not completely separate from even this contemporary saga. Besides the connection in investment principle (valuation insanity and corporate egos are a very, very bad substitute for prudent capital return to shareholders), there is also a literal connection in the chain of events. Consider the timeline:

- In 1989, Time, Inc., merged with Warner Communications, essentially merging the *Time* and *Life* magazine properties (which included *Sports Illustrated*, *People*, and *Fortune*, but also the HBO cable channel) with Warner Bros. (film/TV/music).

---

1 The Bahnsen Group, "What to Learn from the Worst Business Deal in History," *Dividend Cafe*, July 18, 2025, https://thebahnsengroup.com/dividend-cafe/what-to-learn-from-the-worst-business-deal-in-history-july-18-2025/.

- In 1996, Time Warner acquired Turner Broadcasting (CNN, TNT, TBS, the MGM film library, and more).
- In 2000, that Time Warner conglomerate was acquired by AOL, a company generating not even half of the recurring earnings of the acquired company, in a deal that was priced at 100x pro forma earnings, if one is being nice to the accounting, and 300x that pro forma earnings, if one is doing math the way human beings do it.
- In 2009, the deal was fully and completely undone, resulting in two separate companies (much of it had already been undone, sold off, and shed, but I don't want to get too into the weeds).
- In 2018, AT&T acquired what was left of Time Warner's media assets.
- In 2022, AT&T spun off Time Warner and merged it with Discovery, creating the company "Warner Bros. Discovery."
- Under the 2025 deal Netflix has entered into with Warner Bros., the company will "spin off" the legacy properties of CNN, Discovery Channel, TNT, and TBS into a separate company called Discovery Global. That piece of the deal is being priced at something around $0. Zero. Zilch. Now, that is not literally true. But again, in the interest of staying out of the weeds, this spin-off would have negative equity after debt assignment. Regardless of how exactly they slice it up, and where it trades in public markets (if all this ends up happening), this

is essentially a "call option" in the deal with little, no, or negative equity value.

By my count, there are seven mergers of massive companies described above, each with iconic value and brand significance, and, in the end, a major part of the final result is worth $0. Of course, there are other assets at play here, but even if we look at the complete and total picture, AT&T paid $108 billion for something it sold for $43 billion. That spin-off company lost money every year and is now being bought by Netflix.

The shareholders of the merged Time, Warner, and Turner companies were crushed in the AOL deal. The splinters of what was left became a standalone company (ticker: TWX) that had one season of actual operating performance and financial performance bliss: 2010 through 2018. What did TWX do in this period of just being a normal company, growing, creating, marketing, and operating like a real business? It doubled the quarterly dividend from $0.21/share to $0.40/share in six years (11.3 percent annualized dividend growth), and, lo and behold, the company's market cap more than doubled in that period (from $35 billion to $77 billion).

Note, by the way, that the $77 billion of nearly a decade ago is more than the value of the company now at Netflix's current offer.

Steady, organic dividends as management run a growing business: shareholders make a fortune, receive cash, de-risk their investment, and participate as a minority owner in the profits of some of the best media content assets in the world.

Wild M&A deals, mergers with hot internet companies, payments to shareholders are eliminated, money is set on fire, the acquiring companies have to cut their own legacy dividends, and the shareholders of the acquired companies lose both cash flow and underlying value.

Sounds great, right? Well, before you think it was all bad, at least think about the investment bankers and lawyers on all these deals. They have families to feed too. (Total fees across these transactions exceed $1.2 billion, not even counting the current deal with Netflix.)

A PARAMOUNT UNDERSTANDING

I recently read *The King of Content* by Keach Hagey about the life and legacy of Sumner Redstone. Last year, I read *Unscripted* by James B. Stewart about the same subject. While some may find the whole saga of Redstone and his family drama to be fascinating because of the, well, tawdry details, the court battles, the dysfunctional relationships, and the utterly bizarre (and often downright disgusting) dynamics that are paramount to the entire story (see what I did there?), I have studied this whole case study in business history for one reason, and one reason only: what it teaches us about business and investing.

Paramount is as legendary a studio as Hollywood has ever had or will have. In 1966, it was acquired by Gulf & Western, a multisector conglomerate. In 1994, under new management after Gulf & Western's longtime founder and CEO, Charles Bluhdorn, died, the company was sold to Viacom (which was by then owned and controlled by Sumner Redstone, who used an inherited family interest in drive-in movie theaters to leverage his way to buy Viacom in 1987). Viacom owned and operated MTV, Nickelodeon, and Showtime. The 1994 acquisition of Paramount gave Viacom a premier Hollywood studio, the Simon & Schuster book publishing behemoth, several amusement parks and sports venues, and a 50 percent ownership stake in the USA Network. Viacom paid a stunning $10 billion for Paramount in 1994 after winning a bidding war with Barry Diller, allowing us, once and for all, to define "winning" very differently than people who do regular math define it.

In 2000, Redstone's Viacom/Paramount would buy the major television network CBS. In 2006, it split CBS and Paramount into two separate companies, and, in 2019, it re-merged the two. In 2025, the combined Paramount/CBS company was sold to Skydance for $6.6 billion (while also injecting a fresh $1.5 billion of primary equity capital into the company). Now, the company also has $15 billion in net debt, so the total enterprise value is closer to $23 billion. But I just want to be clear: CBS was bought at a $35 billion valuation twenty-five years ago, and Paramount was bought at a $10 billion valuation thirty-two years ago. There is much adjustment to do here to get a perfect apples-to-apples comparison, and some of these deals merging companies with stock swaps make it tricky, but what we can say here is that more than $10 billion of value has been set on fire, at the bare minimum, over a period of twenty-five years. This has not happened with failing companies, but successful, profitable, brand-name enterprises—what I previously referred to as "household names."

DOING THE MATH

Last summer, when these mergers and acquisitions began, I tasked TBG Equity Analyst Ishan Chhabra with analyzing the lifetime return for a Viacom shareholder since the early 1990s. The frequent mergers, splits, and combined entities made it necessary to calculate period returns for five different periods and create an apples-to-apples analysis of a combined, total return for a hypothetical investor over the entire period. When all was said and done, Ishan's brilliant analysis found that investors throughout this whole saga (coinciding, might I add, with the greatest bull market in human history) had a total holding period return of -21.14 percent.

As Ishan so eloquently put it:

> From 1990 through 2025, Viacom's corporate strategy of aggressive M&A activity fundamentally failed to generate shareholder value, culminating into a -21.1% total shareholder return based on a hypothetical investment in late 1993. Research reveals a consistent degradation in share price over the 35 years. The steepest drawdown occurred over a period of merging, splitting, then re-merging with CBS Corporation. The 2005 split, motivated by internal corporate conflicts and perceived operational complexity, fragmented synergies and created two weaker entities that struggled independently for over a decade. The eventual 2019 re-merger, rather than resolving these structural issues, occurred at precisely the wrong moment—coinciding with the onset of the brutal streaming wars that demanded massive capital investments with uncertain returns.

> Then, between 2019–2025, ViacomCBS/Paramount Global's stock price collapsed by approximately 70%, driven by unsustainable streaming losses, cord-cutting acceleration, and management's failure to execute a coherent digital transformation strategy. The following analysis, along with an event-driven walkthrough of a hypothetical portfolio establishment, demonstrates how corporate restructuring decisions, when divorced from operational realities and market timing, can systematically destroy decades of shareholder value creation.

Now, let me make things much worse. The $1,000 hypothetical investment turning into $788 over thirty-two years includes $442 in dividends paid over thirty-two years. In other words, this failure of a company was much, much, much worse of a failure when divorced from the paltry capital it did actually return to its own risk-taking investors.

But as we shall soon see, their refusal to pay dividends is not just a problem because less cash went to investors in calculating their total return. It is, itself, a major source of the fundamental problem.

COMPARE AND CONTRAST

We can look at failed media companies like AOL–Time Warner and Viacom/Paramount/CBS all we want, but has the entire sector failed? Has anything in media content and distribution failed? Of course not. Indeed, how has a company like, say, Comcast (ticker: CMCSA—TBG does not and has never owned this name) compounded at 13 percent per year for the same thirty-two years that Viacom/Paramount blew itself up?

To quote Ishan's research again (emphasis is mine):

> Financial discipline represented perhaps the most critical difference between the two companies' approaches. *Comcast maintained consistent dividend policies* and share repurchase programs throughout its expansion phase, *ensuring that shareholders benefited from cash generation even during major acquisition periods.* The company used debt prudently, maintaining investment-grade credit ratings and *avoiding the over-leveraging* that characterized Viacom's major deals. This financial conservatism provided operational flexibility that proved essential during industry disruption, enabling Comcast to invest in broadband infrastructure upgrades and streaming technology *without compromising core business operations or shareholder returns.*

My point here is not to tout or celebrate Comcast, which is not even a name we have been invested in. It is to use it as an illustration of a much broader point: companies that respect their shareholders enough to maintain a growing dividend while they invest in needed infrastructure, while they ride out tough cyclical times, and while they pursue acquisitions, have an embedded governor of responsibility, prudence, and, dare I say, survival.

For the past twenty years or so, Comcast has grown its dividend by 19.7 percent per year. Paramount/Viacom/CBS shrunk it by 9 percent per year. Yep, one company eroded its dividend year over year over year, while another grew it generously and prudently.

THE HEART OF THE MATTER

Let me hit the point home with a final punch from Ishan's research:

> The most fundamental difference between the two companies is their approach to shareholder capital allocation and investor relations. Comcast maintained a consistent philosophy of returning capital to shareholders throughout its expansion phase, treating dividend payments and share repurchases as essential components of total shareholder return rather than optional expenses during growth periods. This approach demonstrated management's confidence in the underlying business model and ensured that shareholders participated directly in cash flow generation even during major acquisition cycles. The consistency of these returns created investor trust that supported higher valuation multiples and lower cost of capital, providing Comcast with strategic advantages in competitive situations. In stark contrast, Viacom's leadership repeatedly sacrificed dividend policy and share repurchases to fund acquisitions, signaling to investors that management prioritized empire-building over shareholder value creation. This approach eroded investor confidence over time, contributing to valuation discounts that made subsequent transactions

more expensive and reduced strategic flexibility during critical industry transitions.

We are not talking about media companies that make bad decisions, or bad shows, or are late to streaming, or hire bad executives, or get caught in sexual harassment scandals, or have governance problems. Well, okay, we are not *only* talking about those things. What we have here is the most basic of investment lessons I have learned in twenty-five years:

- The dividend is a sign of management's confidence in their own business decisions and business model.
- The dividend is a reward for a good business model that, itself, creates a lower cost of capital for capital-intensive businesses.
- The dividend is a governor of boardroom egos and, in some cases, psychopathic decisions that destroy shareholder value while narcissists pursue delusions of grandeur.

The *Dividend Cafe* would become a historical journal if all I ever wrote about were documented cases of the latter in corporate history.

CONCLUSION

I write regularly about the reality of human nature in investing decisions. I want to assure readers that corporate managers, founders, tycoons, and even board members are also human beings—and also subject to the demons of nature. We accept the constrained vision of reality that the shortcomings of human nature force upon us. And we seek to mitigate that reality with as many tools as we can to optimize our results. In dividend growth investing, we not only get an embedded mitigator of our own human nature (resistance to euphoria and crowd-chasing, and the automatic reinvestment of dividends in inevitable bad times), but also a mitigator of the human nature that plagues corporate managers too. Media companies are not unique. The temptation to do bad things with someone else's money is real. The prudence of returning capital to those who took risks is a game changer.

And history will not stop telling that story.

ABOUT THE BAHNSEN GROUP

FOUNDED IN 2015 AS STAND-ALONE entity, The Bahnsen Group (TBG) previously existed inside UBS (2001–2007) and Morgan Stanley (2007–2014). David and his team at Morgan Stanley left to launch TBG with $600 million in client assets. As this book went to press, The Bahnsen Group managed more than $9.5 billion in client assets, had ninety-six employees (including twenty-four wealth advisors), and twelve offices in:

Newport Beach, CA
New York, NY
Minneapolis, MN
Nashville, TN
Bend, OR
Austin, TX
Dallas, TX
Phoenix, AZ
West Palm Beach, FL
Grand Rapids, MI
Silicon Valley, CA

Pittsburgh, PA

The firm offers comprehensive tax services (planning and return preparation), financial and estate planning, and multi-asset investment solutions. It takes pride in highly personal relationships with each client, and manages money with a customized and tailored approach across the seven building blocks of a portfolio that are its focus.

For more information, visit the website using this QR Code:

Information about the TBG Dividend Focus
Fund (ticker: TBG) can be found here:

ACKNOWLEDGMENTS

IT HAS BEEN TRUE OF every book I have written, but is more true of this book than any other (or so it seems): This book would not have been possible without the loving and sacrificial support of my wife of twenty-five years, Joleen. I certainly mean that in the context of her support for me taking dozens upon dozens of weekend hours to write the book, but I also mean it in the context of my entire career, life, and being. She holds me up when I am about to fall, and she loves me and supports me in a way that transcends what is par for the course in a marriage. She is the best office designer in America, a remarkable mother and friend, and a true leader inside The Bahnsen Group. In fact, she is the heart of TBG. But beyond all that, she is my partner and best friend, and there is no TBG, let alone this book, without her.

This book would also have a very bad title if not for her. This is now the second book in a row where the title was workshopped by her as she and I went on a long walk together.

The dedication to Tom Bonds captures my affection for this stalwart of a human being whom I love like a brother. It doesn't say how lucky Morgan Stanley is to have him, or how lucky the advisors he has managed are to have him in their corner. Tom and I have some scars we earned together, from the financial crisis to various personal journeys that mark who we are as men. I am blessed beyond words to have the shared experiences I have with him, and blessed that God preserved him through a heart attack, not only so that he could continue being the remarkable husband, father, and grandfather that he is, but also so that he and I may continue laughing together. Because we do have a lot to laugh about. And Julie, Joleen, and I love you too!

This book is about dividend growth investing, and Lowell Miller was my mentor, teacher, and friend as I became a dividend growth disciple and, eventually, evangelist. I remain in his debt for his extraordinary legacy as a dividend growth guru.

Nick Murray has been my mentor and friend for twenty-five years now, and has affected me in ways I fear he will never fully understand. The entire financial advisory industry in America (and worldwide) is better because of him.

The dividend growth investing we do at The Bahnsen Group is not a sole individual effort. My partner for many years, Brian Szytel, has been a friend and warrior in the cause, and a highly capable co-CIO. Kenny Molina has built an extraordinary Investment Solutions Department, along with gifted leaders Manuel Ramirez and Eddie Molina. Our analyst team is phenomenal and a driving force in what we do as dividend growth managers. Liping Ouyang is a first-rate talent on this front, and Ishan Chhabra is going to do tremendous things in his career at TBG too.

I am grateful to Luke Theeuwes, Steve Chun, and the whole team at Focus Distribution, as well as Kevin Dinh, and all the good folks at ETF Architect for their support of our dividend strategy ETF (ticker: TBG).

It is a privilege to count the team at Hightower Advisors and THL as partners and friends. Larry, Dan, Gurinder, Matthias, Scott, Barry, Cheryl, Jill, Ganesh, Ed, Bob, Barrett, Shannon, and more—thank you.

John Mauldin has long been a valued resource, and he has become a true partner, advocate, and friend.

Jerry and Susan Bowyer and the whole team at Bowyer Research are fighting the good fight and define what it means to be selfless and happy warriors. Their work in shareholder engagement and proxy voting is creating dividends for their stakeholders, and I mean that both metaphorically and literally. Our companies are worth more—*actually* worth more—because of their fine work.

Fred Whitaker, Ashley Boluc, and Erick Becker at Cummins & White are remarkable lawyers and advocates. They have made us a better company and we are thankful.

My entire leadership team and "steering committee" at The Bahnsen Group are confidants, friends, and partners. As it pertains to this book, in particular, Trevor Cummings provided valuable counsel and was the only person I shared the manuscript with as I was writing. I already mentioned Joleen's and Brian's role in our firm's leadership. Joe Klein and Luis Garcia have kept our trains running across departments and business functions. Together we make a cohesive and united group and have built something we are all proud of.

The Bahnsen Group team is too large, now, for me to mention each person by name. Additionally, we will no doubt have numerous new names by the time this book is released, and so I wouldn't want to leave anyone out if the intention was to be comprehensive. I mention Leadership and key folks from the Investment team here by name because of their specific role with the subject of this book. I also will call out Mina Widmer for the plethora of chart design she has provided for this book, but also the book cover work she and Joleen did together. And our Digital Content group, Brian Tong, Glen Hall, and Lukas Klause, who handled the audio recording and editing (for the fifth book in a row), and also drive our content execution across the firm with patience and precision.

But for the entire TBG family, I love you all. Joleen and I remain relentlessly committed to your success.

Mitchell, Sadie, and Graham, you are the pride and joy of my life. No dividends have ever been more rewarding than the three of you.

My editor, Karina Rollins, did remarkable work in an impressive fashion to fix what I did wrong. What you read here in this book is better because of her, and I am grateful.

Last, but not least, I am so incredibly grateful for the support and friendship of Anthony Ziccardi and his entire team at Post Hill Press. Anthony believed in me as an author before anyone else did, and publishing each book with Post Hill has reaped many dividends that I didn't think possible. Near the top of the list of those dividends has been the friendship Joleen and I now share with Anthony and Katherine. I can't imagine publishing a book with anyone but Post Hill, and I am grateful for your support, advocacy, and friendship.

ABOUT THE AUTHOR

Photo Credit: Alice Gherasim

DAVID L. BAHNSEN is the founder, managing partner, and chief investment officer of The Bahnsen Group, a private wealth management firm managing over $9 billion in client capital. David was a senior portfolio manager and managing director at Morgan Stanley until 2015, at which time he started The Bahnsen Group with eight employees and $600 million in client assets. Today the firm has one hundred employees, twelve offices, and has organically grown assets and revenues at 30 percent per year for over a decade. He is a frequent guest on Fox Business, CNBC, and Bloomberg. He writes weekly at www.dividendcafe.com and is the host of the popular *Capital Record* podcast. He is consistently named one of the top wealth advisors in the country by *Barron's* and *Forbes*.

David and his wife, Joleen, have been married for twenty-five years. They have three children, Mitchell, Sadie, and Graham, and live bi-coastally in New York City and Newport Beach.